The Story of
THE DOUGHBOYS

The Story of
THE DOUGHBOYS
The AEF in World War I

by
Laurence Stallings

Condensed and adapted by
M. S. Wyeth, Jr.,
from *The Doughboys*

Introduction by Hanson W. Baldwin

HARPER & ROW, PUBLISHERS   NEW YORK

Contents

A 16-page section of illustrations follows page 78.

Maps

The map on page xi is from *World War I* by Hanson W. Baldwin.
All other maps are by Harry Scott.

Introduction

by Hanson W. Baldwin

THE WORLD OF 1914—the twilight of the so-called Golden Age of Kings and Empires—died with "the guns of August" when German troops invaded Belgium and drove deep into France.

World War I was the end of an epoch. Monarchies and empires vanished in its maelstrom; kings and princes were overthrown; a whole generation of the bravest and the best died in battle. The Austro-Hungarian empire dissolved in ultimate defeat; the German Kaiser fled to a wood-chopping retirement in Holland; Czar Nicholas II of Russia and his family were murdered by the Bolsheviks. Marxism swept Russia and opened a world conflict between Communist totalitarianism and democratic freedom that still continues. New nations were created from the ruins of the Austro-Hungarian and Russian empires, among them Poland, Czechoslovakia, Austria, and Hungary. The war marked the beginning of the decline of England's greatness. Much of the vigor of the European continent was sapped by the bloodletting. Economically, politically, psychologically, and militarily the transference of power from the Old World to the New commenced.

The statistics of death have never been exceeded save in World War II, which was an outgrowth of World War I. Almost nine million men died in the more than four years of struggle. Millions of civilians died as a result of the disease, pestilence, and famine that stalked in the red wake of war. World War I changed forever the history of our times, and even today its effects go marching on.

It is difficult for the modern generation to imagine the more leisurely world of 1914. At the beginning of the twentieth century the Technological Revolution was still in swaddling clothes. The internal combustion engine and electronic communications were just beginning to influence the world. The Wright brothers had first flown at Kitty Hawk only a few years before the war started. No one had heard and few had even dreamed of atomic power. There was no air transportation; it took months to go around the world, days or weeks to travel to Europe or across the United States. There was no television, no radio broadcasting. The pace of life was slowed, the tempo far less frenetic than it is today.

The soldiers of the day were footsloggers, the artillery horse-drawn; supply depended upon steam railroads and coal-burning ships, and, fundamentally, upon horse-drawn transport. There were few military airplanes and most of those were thought to be of limited use for reconnaissance purposes. The British Navy still ruled supreme upon the seas with one of the greatest fleets in history.

It was an era of empire and of colonies, in Britain's case of an empire upon which the sun never set. Germany, France, Great Britain, and other European powers governed colonial possessions in Africa. The Far East was dominated by Europe and by an ambitious and growing Japan; China was a stage for great power rivalries.

This world of long ago (separated from us by a short space of time historically, but by an immense gulf technologically) was profoundly different in every way from modern society—save for one element, Man himself.

And it was Man—Man in the collective—with all his faults and virtues, all his strengths and weaknesses, that was responsible for the outbreak of World War I.

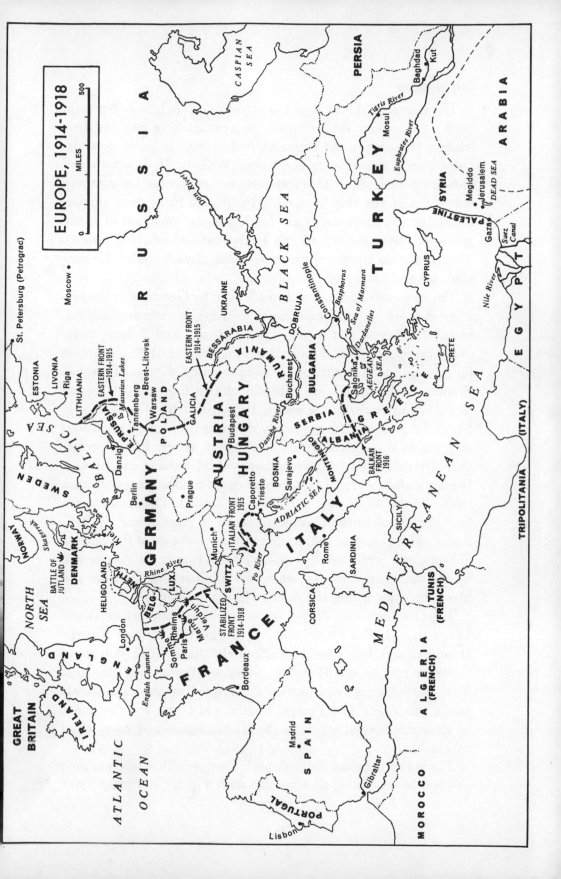

Introduction

The causes of World War I are rooted deep in history but stem from the ambitions, the strengths, the weaknesses of men and their leaders. Germany under Bismarck had become in a few short decades a great world power, but Kaiser Wilhelm II, an erratic and bombastic ruler given to impetuous outbursts, was an unsteady helmsman of the ship of state. The Austro-Hungarian empire, under the old Emperor Franz Josef, was an amalgam of many races and nationalities and was in the twilight of its greatness. The autocratic Russia of the czars was already roiled by conspiracies and attempted revolutions.

The empire of England was challenged by Germany in the prewar years—in banking supremacy, in trade, in industrial output, in naval strength, and in colonial ambitions. And France, bitter over her defeat in the Franco-Prussian War of 1870, hungered for revenge and the return of her lost provinces of Alsace-Lorraine. France and England were naturally drawn together in reaction to the rising power of Germany. Italy, ruled by a weak king— Victor Emmanuel III—was newly emerged from ancient divisions and was avid to be recognized as a great power. In the prewar years Italy signed a defensive alliance with Germany and Austria-Hungary, but when the stakes were down she reneged, then shifted to the Allied side after the war started. The Balkans, the "powder keg of Europe," were the scene of great power rivalries. Austria-Hungary was anxious to expand its empire at the expense of Serbia; the Serbs, tied by Pan-Slavism to Russia and encouraged by the czar, hoped for a Greater Serbia to include Serbian and Slav minorities within the Austro-Hungarian empire.

Thus the lines were drawn, the sides chosen long before World War I started. The Triple Alliance, originally Germany, Austria-Hungary, and Italy, became ultimately the Central Powers of Germany and Austria-Hungary, joined by Turkey and Bulgaria. To this combination was opposed the Triple Entente (later loosely called "the Allies") of France, Russia, and Great Britain, joined by Belgium, Serbia, and later the United States and many other nations.

The storm that was to break over Europe in that summer long ago had been building up more and more rapidly ever since 1900.

There had been crises after crises—among them two Moroccan crises when the colonial ambitions of Germany and France clashed (in 1905 and 1911), in the Balkans in 1908 when Serbian and Russian interests collided with those of Austria-Hungary, in two Balkan wars (Serbia against Turkey in 1912 and Serbia against Bulgaria in 1913), and in other less serious incidents. Italy's colonial ambitions also led to a brief war with Turkey (1911–1912) which resulted in Italian occupation of the Dodecanese islands and of Tripolitania and Cyrenaica in North Africa. Statesmen—then as now—seemed powerless to avert Armageddon. Lord Grey, the British Foreign Secretary who had forged the Triple Entente, was an exemplar of a pallid diplomacy, while the Kaiser thundered and blundered.

Many books have been written assessing the causes of World War I, apportioning blame and allocating failures. There were commercial and industrial and political and economic rivalries, weak rulers, shortsighted policies, clashing colonial ambitions, ethnic and national rivalries, an arms race, and other causes. But fundamentally, as in all wars, the cause was the nature of Man himself.

The immediate spark was the assassination of the heir to the Austrian throne, Archduke Francis Ferdinand, at Sarajevo on June 28, 1914. By August the Old World was at war. In quick succession the great powers of Europe marched into the conflict, with Germany and Austria-Hungary fighting Serbia, Russia, Belgium, Luxembourg, France, and the British Empire. By midnight August 4 Europe was engaged in a war which was to dwarf even the Napoleonic wars.

The two major battlegrounds at the beginning of the war were the Western Front, in northern France and southwest Belgium, and the Eastern Front, from the Black Sea to the Baltic. German hopes for a quick victory over France were based on the Schlieffen plan. The strategy called for a strong German offensive in the West, with a sweeping movement through Belgium and Luxembourg to outflank French fortifications and troops and to wheel around Paris, and a temporary German defense against Russia in the East. The Schlieffen plan might have succeeded; it almost did, but a combination of mistakes by German generals and magnificent French defenses resulted in the Battle of the Marne, a decisive battle in which the German armies were repulsed short of Paris and recoiled in retreat.

The retreat was followed by a series of battles that lasted throughout the waning months of 1914—the Battle of the Aisne, then the "race to the sea," with each side trying to outflank the other and reach the English Channel ports. This phase of the war ended in the First Battle of Ypres, a name hallowed in British memory. The British Expeditionary Force and Belgian and French troops barely stemmed the German tide. But they did stem it and by the end of 1914 the war in the West had assumed the character it was to retain through more than four long years of bloody struggle—a static front with armies bogged down in trench systems and dugouts behind snarls of barbed wire. This was the beginning of a system of continuous field fortifications that were to become more and more elaborate and that were to defy conquest by either side until the closing months of the war.

The vast Eastern Front, where Russian, German, and Austro-Hungarian forces faced each other with millions of men, was somewhat less thickly held, but even there trench systems and fortified areas played major roles in the ebb and flow of battle. In the early months of the war the Germans crushed the Russians in a tremendous campaign at Tannenberg and the Masurian lakes on the border of East Prussia. The Russians lost 300,000 men before the war was two months old and, many later thought, suffered a blow from which they never fully recovered.

As the war continued, the number of nations involved constantly expanded. Japan, wanting the Asian spoils of Germany's colonial empire, had joined the Allies in late August, 1914. With negligible fighting the Japanese took over German-held Tsingtao in China and the German islands in the Pacific. Turkey, then known as the Ottoman Empire, joined the Central Powers in October, 1914. For three years Turkey waged a series of bloody campaigns against Russia on their mutual border and fought British colonial forces for control of the Middle East and the strategic Suez Canal. Italy entered the war in May, 1915, on the side of the Allies. A new front was formed against the Austro-Hungarians from the Adriatic Sea to Switzerland. This front, like the Western Front, quickly became deadlocked and virtually static. Rumania, hungry for spoils, joined the Allies in 1916. Africa became engulfed in the flames of war. The shot fired at Sarajevo, like a stone thrown into a pond, roiled the depths of nations, races, social systems, and continents.

On the Western Front generals of both sides tried again and again to break the deadlock of trench warfare in a series of bloody battles—Ypres, St. Mihiel, Loos, Vimy Ridge, the Champagne, Verdun, the Somme, and the Aisne. The only result was a few yards or miles of shell-pocked ground gained and millions of lives lost. By 1917 the French army, bled white, was exhausted and mutinous. The Russians and Austro-Hungarians were in little better shape. The ebb and flow of the war over the 1,150-mile Eastern Front had covered much greater areas of ground, but the results had been the same: millions killed, wounded, or captured, but no decisive victories by either side. By the time the United States entered the war, the Austro-Hungarian empire was reeling, the czar of Russia had abdicated, and revolution raged in St. Petersburg. (By March of 1918 the Russian Revolution was complete and Russia formally withdrew from the war.)

In addition to the two main fronts bloody fighting continued between Italians and Austro-Hungarians. In an attempt to bypass the trench stalemate on the Western Front the British, with Australian, New Zealand, and French help, opened a new front in 1915 on the Turkish peninsula of Gallipoli. The objective was to capture the Dardanelles, open a sea passage to the Russian Black Sea ports, and force Turkey out of the war. The campaign almost succeeded, but temporizing and hesitant British field leadership and courageous and determined resistance by Germans and Turks defeated the attempt. In the fall of 1915 Serbia was knocked out of the war by a pincer offensive from Bulgaria and Austria-Hungary.

Other fronts were opened by the Allies in Greece and in the Middle East. In Mesopotamia, near the Persian Gulf, the British Indian Army and men of many nations fought in the hot sands of the desert. In 1916 and 1917 fighting in the Middle East expanded from the Suez Canal and Sinai campaign to Palestine. General Sir Edmund Allenby, aided by groups of Arab irregulars led by an erratic genius—Lawrence of Arabia—fought the beleaguered Turks, who were assisted by a handful of Germans. The Turks, weakened by the Gallipoli campaign and endless fighting against the Russians in the Caucasus and the British in Mesopotamia, were finally overwhelmed. Baghdad and then Jerusalem were taken, and ultimately the decadent Turkish empire, which had outlasted its time, fell apart in the ruck of defeat.

Throughout all the years of the war until after the final armistice in Europe, a dramatic sideshow in German East Africa pitted a wily and elusive German officer, Lettow-Vorbeck, with chiefly native troops, against British, Belgian, and colonial forces. The German campaign was a minor masterpiece; the British ultimately won German East Africa, but Lettow-Vorbeck remained at large until the end—a menace to the conquerors.

At sea World War I was dominated by two factors: the British superiority in surface ships and the German submarine campaign. The Germans challenged, but only sporadically and ineffectively, the British naval superiority on the surface. One of the greatest naval battles in history took place in the North Sea in 1916 off the Danish peninsula. The Battle of Jutland resulted in heavy losses to both sides, considerably more for the British than the Germans. It was a tactical and moral victory for Germany but a strategic victory for Britain; the British still held the seas. German surface raiders and clashes between far-flung cruiser squadrons provided drama, but did little to influence fundamentally the course of the war.

The British naval blockade of Germany and her allies had slow effect, but in time it contributed materially to the German defeat. It hurt German morale and caused shortages of food and raw materials. But in turn the German submarine campaign against merchant shipping blockaded Britain and almost defeated her.

The unrestricted warfare of the German submarines, which resulted in the loss of American lives in torpedoed ships, was one of the direct causes of American entry into the war. The submarine campaign, the invasion of Belgium, the attack upon Serbia, and the carefully nurtured tales, most of them untrue or exaggerated, of fiendish German atrocities provided the emotional tinder which helped to bring the United States into the war and to tilt the balance against the Kaiser.

The German submarines almost, but not quite, destroyed the bridge of ships to England and from England to the continent, upon which the supply of armies and the course of the war depended. When the United States entered the war in the spring of 1917, the loss of merchant shipping had become so serious that Admiral John Jellicoe, British First Sea Lord, reported that it "is impossible for us to go on with the war if losses like this continue. . . ." The answer was the convoy system, which grouped merchant ships into protected convoys, herded by men-of-war. From the latter half of 1917 onward, shipping losses steadily declined.

In the air the airplane, a sputtering machine of wood and fabric when the conflict started, commenced to come of age about the time the United States declared war. The air fleets of the combatants grew from a few hundred unarmed machines in the opening months of the conflict to more than ten thousand at the end. German seaplanes and zeppelins, and later Gotha and Giant bombers, bombed London, and the genesis of modern air power was written above the mud and blood and rubble of the trenches.

This, then, was the kind of war America entered in April, 1917—a war still stalemated on the Western Front after more than two and a half years of fighting, the antagonists winded and gasping, nations and empires riddled by casualties, revolution stalking the streets of Russia, German submarines sinking ships of all nations in fiery holocausts at sea.

The United States was then a young and largely untested giant of the West. The older nations of Europe, with long martial traditions and years of bitter fighting behind them, tended to look down their noses at American military capabilities. In one way they were right; the United States found that it took time, much time, to build and ship thousands of tons of war materials across the seas. Nearly all the artillery and most of the planes the U.S. forces used in World War I were manufactured and provided by their allies. The United States found that a million men simply cannot "spring to arms overnight," that it takes time to raise troops and to train and organize them. But American shipyards did build a bridge of ships across the Atlantic, and American manpower, straight and tall and vigorous, infused the fading cause of the Allies with new life. The United States did not win World War I but the United States probably saved the Allies from ultimate defeat or stalemate. The cost to the United States in lives and dollars was relatively small, although the nation started then a national debt never since wiped out. To Europe the cost was staggering, catastrophic, but the United States emerged from the flames of conflict as, at least potentially, the most powerful nation on earth.

In this war of tremendous consequence to the history of man, a young and confident Army—the American Expeditionary Force —marched with a lilt in its heart and a song on its lips. It is of this army—the A.E.F., the "Doughboys"—that Laurence Stallings writes in magnificent prose. He was one of them—a young Marine who lost a leg for his country in that first great war so long ago; he is now an old Marine, with both legs gone, and a wheelchair as his throne, but he has the same brave spirit which typified the A.E.F. of 1917–1918.

Stallings' tribute to the A.E.F. has been long in the making, but it has been seasoned by memories and nostalgia, study and research.

The author has brought to this history the same spirit the Doughboys brought to World War I—the spirit of a crusade, the spirit of youth, the spirit of vigor.

It was this spirit—an aura of élan, a sense of confidence, a certainty of victory—that those tall young soldiers from the cities and the plains of the Western world brought to France in 1917.

And it is perhaps this spirit, when all is said and done, that will live in history and that was probably the greatest contribution of the United States to the victory in World War I.

Chapter

1

The First Arrivals

FEW GREAT MOMENTS in American history have been as inconspicuous as the arrival of the first American soldiers in France. They came ashore at ten o'clock on the sunny morning of June 13, 1917, at Boulogne-sur-Mer, a pleasant resort on the English Channel. There was no fanfare about their arrival. They had crossed from England by Channel steamer, heavily escorted against German submarines. The group, an advance guard of 177 staff officers and aides, consisted of generals, colonels, majors, captains, lieutenants, sergeants—and very few riflemen. They were led by Major General John J. Pershing.

These Yank soldiers, the first ever sent to Europe to fight, were the advance guard of a United States army that was getting ready to take part in World War I. The war had already been raging on the continent for three years, and the Yanks were joining the Allies—the French and the British—in their fight against the German and Austrian empires.

In August of 1914 Germany and Austria had sent their powerful armies into Belgium and France, and one by one the other major powers of Europe—Russia, England, Turkey, and Italy—

1

and many lesser ones, were drawn into the fight. The United States made every effort to remain neutral from the beginning. But German aggression in starting the war, and especially her unprovoked and brutal invasion of little Belgium, turned many Americans against Germany. In 1916 the German government, in an effort to cut off supplies from England and France, ordered German submarines to sink any ships approaching or leaving the French and British coasts. These unrestricted submarine attacks against unarmed merchant ships of all nations caused the loss of a number of American ships and lives and were a direct violation of the long-established principle of "freedom of the seas." American President Woodrow Wilson warned Germany that, if the attacks continued, the United States would be forced to act. When Germany ignored the warning and more American lives were lost in the early months of 1917, the President asked Congress for a declaration of war. In Wilson's words, America would send an army to France that was "going to make the world safe for democracy."

When the United States declared war on Germany and Austria on April 6, 1917, the country was completely unprepared. There was only a small Regular Army, and there was an inadequate supply of rifles, artillery, and other military necessities. Nevertheless, many Americans thought that six weeks of American action would be enough to defeat the German military machine. Patriotism ran high, and thousands of young men rushed to enlist in the armed forces. But President Wilson and his advisers knew that a great effort would be required before America's armed might would be large and strong enough to make a real contribution, and they promptly set to work. A draft law was enacted to guarantee adequate manpower. Training camps were hastily built and staffed with Regular soldiers whose job it would be to train the newcomers. Factories were converted and expanded for the production of uniforms and vast amounts of other military supplies. All of this required money, far more than had ever been raised before by the government, but Congress willingly appropriated the funds. Yet in spite of all the planning, hard work, and goodwill, it soon became apparent that it would take many months for a sizable force to be recruited, armed, trained, and then sent across the ocean. As we have seen, it was two months before even General Pershing and his advance guard arrived in France.

No one knew better than Pershing how small and ill-equipped the Regular Army was. He had just completed a tour of duty with several units along the Rio Grande, where his soldiers had picked up a nickname, "Doughboys," that would stick to them through World War I and become as distinctive for that era as "G.I." would become for American soldiers in the Second World War.

On the Rio Grande, U.S. Infantry, powdered white by the dust of the adobe soil found throughout the Southwest, were called "adobes" by mounted troops. It was a short step from "adobes" to "dobies" and then, eventually, to the more familiar "Doughboys."

In 1916 Pershing had led these Doughboys on an expedition into Mexico to break up the bands of Pancho Villa, the Mexican revolutionary leader turned bandit, who had crossed into Columbus, New Mexico, one night and slaughtered the inhabitants. Pershing had been under orders to give a demonstration of American strength, and he had carried out his assignment with competence.

Few Doughboys ever got to know John J. Pershing. He was in every way the Iron Commander that many came to think him, an officer who did not curry favor with his troops. But hundreds of thousands of them would not forget him—ramrod straight, in an impeccable uniform, with his hard eyes and a neat mustache above set, thin lips—as he walked the lines to inspect them. Pershing was the very portrait of a soldier, and he demanded the highest standards of himself and all who served under him. One phrase, repeated three times, comprised his highest compliment to a subordinate. When he said of a man, "He is a fighter," it meant that the fellow, if he stayed alive, might someday win a command. When he said of a colonel, "He is a fighter . . . a fighter!" that colonel was getting a little closer to being promoted to brigadier general. But when he said, "He is a fighter . . . a fighter . . . a

3

fighter!" it was time for that colonel to go out and buy a brigadier general's stars.

Pershing was the oldest of nine children of a Missouri railroad man. At eighteen he was a country schoolteacher who could break a colt, plow a straight furrow, and bark a squirrel with a long rifle. He hoped to be a judge someday. At twenty-two he was working in a cornfield when his younger brother came out to tell him that there was to be a competition for an appointment to West Point. Despairing of ever saving enough money to study for the bar, he dropped his plow handles and resolved to win the appointment. Four years later he was a cavalry shavetail (second lieutenant) fighting Apaches of the Tonto Rim, and after that he became Chief of Scouts for General Nelson Miles in the suppression of an uprising among the North Dakota Sioux. He proved to be a magnificent soldier, and in the Spanish-American War he distinguished himself as the leader of the 10th U.S. Cavalry on San Juan Hill, earning the praise of a veteran of many Civil War battles as "the coolest man under fire I ever saw." Later he served ably as an administrator in the Philippines, handling with firmness and diplomacy the proud, native Moros, who wanted their independence.

Because of his fine record President Wilson and Secretary of War Newton D. Baker had been unanimous in their choice of Pershing to lead the American Expeditionary Force to France. It would have been a difficult assignment for any man, for he had to wear the hats of three men—diplomat, administrator, and fighting general. Baker had such confidence in Pershing that he told him, "I shall give you only two orders, one to go and one to return," and Baker was as good as his word.

On hand to greet Pershing and his men as they walked down the gangplank at Boulogne-sur-Mer that sunny morning of June 13, 1917, were the mayor, government representatives, and a number of important French and British generals whose armies had lost three million men in the two and a half years since the war had begun. France added a gracious personal touch: Colonel Jacques

Adelbert de Chambrun, a descendant of Lafayette, who had served General Washington so well in the American Revolution, presented himself as Pershing's personal aide for the duration of the war. Some heels were clicked, hands touched to visors, and the group set out to tour the city before boarding a train for the French capital.

Paris, the "City of Light," now much subdued by the sorrows of war, was some 175 miles to the east. At this time, the front line, at its closest some seventy miles northeast of Paris, stretched across the fields and forests of northern France and the southwest corner of Belgium from the Swiss border to the English Channel. The French armies, whose gallant soldiers were known as "*poilus*," a French word that means "hairy ones" and that was meant to suggest bearded "he-men," held down the eastern and central portion of the Allied line. The British Expeditionary Force, whose backbone was the courageous "Tommie," defended the left flank in northwestern France and in the southwest corner of Belgium.

Neither the Allied nor German armies had advanced or retreated more than a few miles since the German invasion had been stopped at the end of 1914. German infantry on one side, and French and British infantry on the other, were dug into the ground in an elaborate system of trenches several miles wide. Between them was a neutral area laced with coils of jagged barbed wire and known as no-man's-land, whose width varied from as little as fifty yards in some places to over a mile in others. It was a strange kind of warfare that had developed, a defensive war unlike anything seen before, involving millions of men in strong positions along a four-hundred-mile, nearly stationary front. There was no room for one army to outmaneuver or outflank another; soldiers could only go forward in frontal assaults, and the machine gun, a brand-new weapon, supported by tremendous numbers of heavy artillery, had made such attacks a suicidal venture. As a result, for two and a half years the war in France had been a defensive stalemate.

These facts and many others would be brought home to Pershing and the Yanks in the months ahead, but this day, June 13, 1917, was a day for ceremony. After visiting the sights of Boulogne-sur-Mer, Pershing and his men climbed aboard the Paris train. As the locomotive cheeped its way through some of the loveliest countryside in the world the Yanks unbuttoned the tight collars of their 1917 army blouses, loosened their shoes, and promptly went to sleep. Pershing had been provided with a compartment. Being a practical man, he pulled off his boots, shucked his fashion-plate uniform, and went to bed.

All ranks and grades were aroused in time to alight in Paris, in full uniform, where the people had been alerted by newspaper extras to expect the Yanks and had turned out by the thousands to see them. Among the French politicians and generals at the station to meet them was one whom the Americans, and particularly Pershing, would get to know well in the next eighteen months. He was Major General Ferdinand Foch, a celebrated War College professor of strategy and something of an eccentric, now Chief of the General Staff.

After an exchange of formalities Pershing and his staff were escorted to automobiles for the drive to the Hotel Crillon, where they were to be quartered. Paris had long since lost its gaiety. Three years of grinding sacrifices and terrible losses had brought sadness to nearly every home, and there were many Parisian women who were mourning for a husband, brother, or sweetheart who would never return. Yet thousands had gathered to see the long-awaited Yanks. With difficulty the automobiles made their way through the crowds to the Place de la Concorde and the great facade of the Hotel Crillon. Those who had not been able to touch the automobiles of the cavalcade or catch a glimpse of the Americans, filled the Place de la Concorde like sardines in a can. Pershing was forced again and again to appear on a balcony and face the cheering, curious throng. Perhaps no other man in history had felt as inadequate or as helpless as did Pershing on this day, for he knew how unprepared his country was to deliver, immediately, what the French people had led themselves to expect—a mighty army that would hurl the Germans back to the Rhine.

Once the crowd had been satisfied, Pershing and the rest of the Americans were allowed to retire. For the next few days they would be engaged in a long series of conferences with the French and British, in which they would learn about the state of the war and make plans for American participation.

2

How It Began

T<small>HE</small> <small>AMERICAN</small> <small>ARMY</small> staff officers, lodged in the Crillon to be briefed on the Allies' situation, knew of the Great War mainly from censored accounts published in the newspapers. President Wilson had been firm in insisting on a policy of official neutrality, reflecting a belief that went back to the time of President George Washington, who had urged the young nation to stay out of European entanglements. As recently as 1916 Wilson had campaigned for reelection on the slogan, "He kept us out of war." The result was that, when the United States entered the war six months later, not only was the country unprepared but even the top military men were ignorant of the real situation on the Western Front.

In 1914 the French and the British had been nearly as unaware of what lay ahead as the Americans were to be three years later. Only the Germans and the Austrians had been prepared for a full-scale war. Germany, a young and ambitious nation formed out of twenty-five small states in 1871 under the leadership of Prussia, had been building up her army and navy for several decades. Her emperor, Kaiser Wilhelm II, resented the long-established power and prestige of France, Russia, and England. He wanted to expand Germany's trade and influence, and he wanted to establish German colonies in Africa and Asia, where France and England had been colonial powers for over a century.

To strengthen his position, the Kaiser had formed an alliance with Austria, an alliance that later included Bulgaria and Turkey. After the outbreak of the war these nations became known as the Central Powers.

To protect themselves from the growing German threat, France, England, and Russia had formed the Triple Entente and had promised to come to each other's aid in the event one of them was attacked.

The spark that touched off the conflict was an assassination in the Balkans on June 28, 1914. The victim was the heir to the Austrian throne, the Archduke Francis Ferdinand, shot down while driving through the streets of Sarajevo, the capital of the Austrian province of Bosnia. The assassin was a young Bosnian patriot, Gavrilo Princip, who hoped his deed would help gain independence for his people. The plot was traced to a secret organization in the neighboring country of Serbia, and Austria held Serbia responsible for the outrage. The Austrian government issued an ultimatum to Serbia that virtually demanded Serbia surrender to Austrian rule, and, when the Serbian government refused to comply, Austria declared war on July 28, 1914.

Frantic efforts were made by other European governments to keep the fighting from spreading, but the momentum of events and alliances was too great. Russia regarded the nearby Balkans as her proper sphere of influence and considered the Austrian invasion of Serbia as a dangerous threat. The Russian czar began to call up his army in order to come to Serbia's aid. Germany felt she could not ignore this Russian threat to her Austrian ally, and so she declared war on Russia. France and England were drawn in by reason of their alliance with Russia and declared war on Germany in the first week of August.

When the news flashed around the continent that the war had really begun, many people were caught up in the excitement and were relieved that the weeks of uncertainty were over. A few realized what the outbreak of war really meant. In London Sir Edward Grey, Secretary of Foreign Affairs, remarked to his wife, "The lights are going out all over Europe." It was true; after a century of relative peace, of growing optimism that war could be avoided by civilized people, Europe was about to plunge into the worst war in its history, and the world would never be the same again.

The war would change the map of Europe drastically and bring about the fall of several monarchies, including Austria, Germany, and Russia, which had influenced events on the continent for many years. It would be largely responsible for the birth of some new European democracies, such as Czechoslovakia, Austria, Hungary, and of the world's first communist state, Soviet Russia.

There were many people who hoped that out of the ashes of the war a new and less troublesome world order could be constructed. President Wilson believed it would be "a war to end war." On the contrary, it created many new problems and sowed the seeds of World War II. Looking back on the First World War we can see that it was a turning point in history, a watershed marking the end of the old order and the dawn of the modern era.

Many years before 1914 Germany's able General Staff had prepared a brilliant strategy in the event she would have to fight simultaneously on her eastern and western borders. The plan was based on the assumption that it would take a huge country like Russia a long time to mobilize her troops and get her armies into the field. Consequently Germany's military leaders decided to leave a small defensive force on the eastern border to prevent a Russian invasion of Prussia and to concentrate Germany's main strength in the west for a quick, all-out attack against France. There, before the small English army could affect the outcome—if it even crossed the Channel—the Germans expected to overwhelm the French in a few weeks. Then, with France conquered, the Germans would move their forces to the Eastern Front and, in cooperation with the large Austrian Army, bring down the slow-moving Russian bear.

The key to Germany's assault in the west was to be surprise. The German General Staff knew that French defenses would be strongest along the two-hundred-mile French-German border, so they proposed to attack swiftly with two million men across neutral Luxembourg and Belgium. While the German left wing faked a direct attack across the French-German border and tied down most of the French forces, the German right wing, with the greatest concentration of strength, would rush through unprepared Belgium, swing south into France, and circle around below Paris, trapping the French armies to the east.

The Germans put this plan—named after its originator, General Alfred von Schlieffen—into operation on August 4, 1914, five weeks after the assassination of the Austrian archduke. Seven armies, four of them facing Belgium and Luxembourg, smashed across the borders. In a burst of confidence General von Moltke, German Chief of Staff, wired the Kaiser, "In six weeks it will all be over." But much to the Germans' surprise—and to the admiration of the world—the small Belgian army put up a spirited fight and managed to delay the Germans several days. At the same time, the Russians mobilized their forces and attacked in East Prussia much sooner than expected, forcing Moltke to transfer four of his western divisions to help defend Germany's eastern border.

Even so, Germany almost won the war in the west as quickly as Moltke had predicted. While the main French armies to the south and east managed to hold the German left wing just inside the frontier, nothing could stop the tremendous power of the German right wing. It broke through the Belgian defenses and raced unopposed into northern France, its infantry marching twenty miles or more a day, its cavalry probing far ahead. The advance guard of the British Expeditionary Force, now supporting the French left flank, made a brave but brief stand at Mons and then retreated. There was nothing the weak and surprised French and British could do but fight brief delaying actions as they fell back toward Paris. Government officials and citizens began to evacuate the capital.

The German right wing was finally stopped in early September,

11

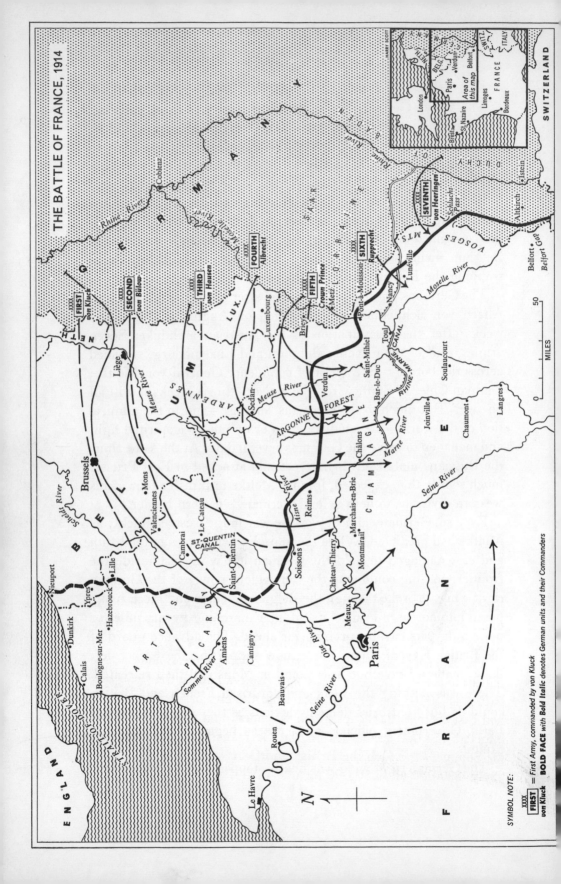

THE BATTLE OF FRANCE, 1914

SYMBOL NOTE:

XXXX
FIRST = First Army, commanded by von Kluck
von Kluck **BOLD FACE** with **Bold Italic** denotes German units and their Commanders

1914. It had been slowed in late August by exhaustion and by confusion and uncertainty among its individual army commanders about their orders. When the two German armies nearest Paris became separated, the French recognized a great opportunity and launched a counterattack in the vicinity of the Marne River. This crucial First Battle of the Marne, one of the greatest battles in history and involving three million men, began on September 5, 1914, and lasted about four days. The tide was turned when Major General Joseph Simon Galliéni, commanding the Paris garrison, rushed up reinforcements in Paris taxicabs, creating one of the great legends of the war. At the battle's end, the German right wing was driven back forty miles to the Aisne River, and Paris was saved.

After their setback at the Marne, the Germans tried to outflank the French and British by slipping around them to the west. But the Allies were trying the same tactics on the Germans, and the result was a race west to the sea that ended in a stalemate in a corner of Belgium on the Channel coast. As 1914 drew to a close, soldiers of both sides dug trenches facing each other and awaited their generals' plans for the future.

The generals' plans were not inspired. They ordered offensives in 1915 and again in 1916, frontal assaults against prepared defenses that changed lines only slightly at the cost of millions of casualties. In 1915 the French lost 125,000 men in an unsuccessful attempt to retake the city of Saint-Mihiel near the French-German border, and another 240,000 in an offensive at the center of the line near the cathedral city of Reims. The British in their turn had lost virtually all of their professional soldiers and most of the new volunteers in suicidal attacks in Flanders.

The American staff officers in the Crillon had read about these battles in the newspapers. They had also read about the two great battles of 1916: the French defense of the city of Verdun, which had cost them 542,000 in killed, wounded, and missing and had inflicted 434,000 casualties on the Germans; and the Battle of the Somme, for which the British and Germans had paid, respectively, 420,000 and 650,000 men.

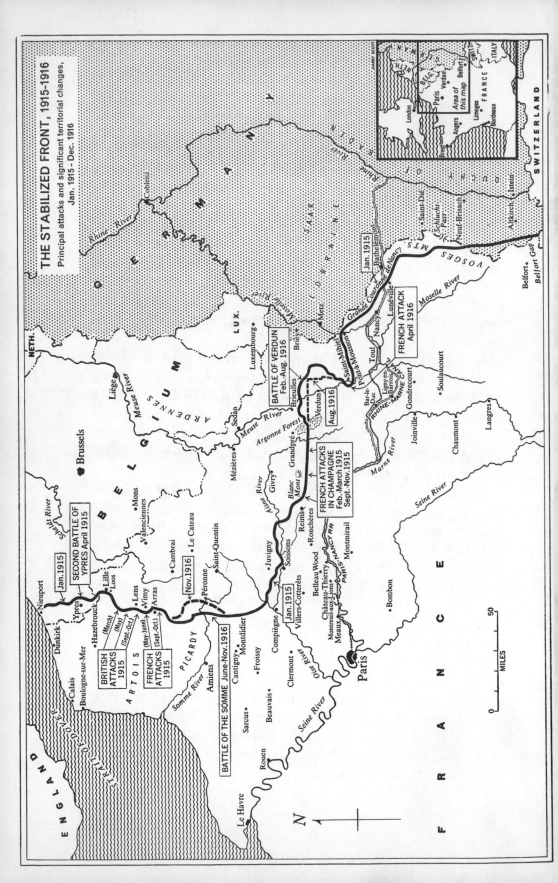

THE STABILIZED FRONT, 1915-1916
Principal attacks and significant territorial changes,
Jan. 1915 - Dec. 1916

ENGLAND

STRAIT OF DOVER

Le Havre

Rouen

Seine River

Dunkirk
Calais
Boulogne-sur-Mer

Nieuport
Jan.1915
SECOND BATTLE OF YPRES April 1915
Ypres
Hazebrouck
Lille
Loos
(March)
(May)
(Sept.-Oct.)
BRITISH ATTACKS 1915
Lens
Vimy
(May-June)
(Sept.-Oct.)
FRENCH ATTACKS 1915
Arras
ARTOIS
PICARDY
Sarcus
Beauvais
Amiens
Somme River
Cantigny
Montdidier
BATTLE OF THE SOMME June-Nov.1916
Nov.1916
Péronne
Saint-Quentin
Le Cateau
Cambrai

Brussels
BELGIUM
Schelde River
Mons
Valenciennes

Liège
Meuse River
Sedan
Mézières
ARDENNES

NETH.
GERMANY
Rhine River
Coblenz

LUX.
Luxembourg
Meuse River

SAAR
LORRAINE
Moselle River
Briey
Metz

Froissy
Clermont
Compiègne
Oise River
Juvigny
Soissons
Aisne River
Givry
Grandpré
Argonne Forest
Blanc Mont
Reims
Ronchères
FRENCH ATTACKS IN CHAMPAGNE Feb.-March 1915 Sept.-Nov.1915
Verdun
Aug.1916
Brieulles
BATTLE OF VERDUN Feb.-Aug. 1916
Saint-Mihiel
Pont-à-Mousson
Grande Couronne de Nancy
Jan.1915
Bathelemont

Villers-Cotterêts
Belleau Wood
Château-Thierry
Montreuil-aux-Lions
Meaux
Montmirail
PARIS-NANCY RR
Paris
Jan.1915

Marne River
Seine River
Bombon

Bar-le-Duc
Ligny-en-Barrois
RHINE-MARNE CANAL
Toul
Nancy
Lunéville
Moselle River
FRENCH ATTACK April 1916
Gondrecourt
Soulaucourt
Joinville
Chaumont
Langres

Saint-Dié
Schluch Pass
VOSGES MTS.
Neuf-Brisach
Altkirch
stein

Belfort
Belfort Gap

DUCHY OF
SWITZERLAND
ITALY

FRANCE

N

MILES
0   50

NETH.
BEL.
London
Paris
Verdun
Angers
Limoges
Bordeaux
Brest
FRANCE
SWITZ.
Belfort
Area of this map
MARY SCOTT

In these battles wave upon wave of infantry had gone forward, climbing out of the trenches in which they lived and took shelter and going "over the top." They cut their way through the coils of jagged barbed wire strung between opposing trenches by using wire clippers, or they blasted a path through the wire with Bangalore torpedoes (steel pipes stuffed with dynamite). Unless it was a sneak attack, the attackers usually followed as closely as possible a creeping artillery barrage from their own guns massed behind their own lines. The guns would fire and, following a precise schedule, the gunners would alter the range of each salvo so that the shells would "walk over" enemy trenches, from no-man's-land to well behind enemy lines. While the rain of shells was falling the enemy had to take shelter. If the attackers could stay "on the heels" of the exploding shells they would be virtually free of enemy fire, and sometimes they could capture an enemy trench before the enemy could regain machine-gun and rifle positions.

Sometimes these assults were successful for the first few thousand yards, but they were always costly. Troops of both sides had learned to go deep underground into dugouts and bombproof shelters the minute a barrage started, reappearing as soon as it passed behind, in time to cut down the attackers with machine-gun fire.

Not one of these enormous offensives had succeeded in breaking through opposing lines into the clear, for both sides had learned to construct row on row of trenches and strong points far behind the front line. By the time the surviving infantry, disorganized and exhausted, had managed to penetrate a mile or two of trench systems, they found themselves subjected to fierce counterattacks and pounded by hostile artillery that rendered the sending up of fresh supplies and replacements virtually impossible.

In desperation both sides had sought an answer to the stalemate with new weapons. The military possibilities of aircraft were recognized in Europe long before they were recognized in the United States, where the Wright brothers had made the world's first flights in 1902. The Allies and the Germans employed airplanes from the beginning of the war. Of flimsy construction and with unpredictable engines, they were used mainly for reconnaissance and artillery spotting until 1915, when the Germans produced a plane with a machine gun synchronized to fire through the propeller. From then until the end of the war German Fokkers, French Spads and Nieuports, and English Sopwith Camels participated in spectacular aerial dogfights and strafed troops on the ground. But the planes were too light to be really useful or effective for bombing, and their influence on the fighting on the ground was minor throughout the war. (The United States never put more than one type of plane of its own into action, the very dangerous de Haviland 4.)

The Germans introduced the use of poison gas in January, 1915, trying it out first on the Russians in Poland before surprising the French and Canadians with it on the Western Front a few months later. It created panic at first, and was used here and there by both sides during the rest of the war. However, gas masks were quickly developed that were able to reduce its effectiveness, and the gas itself proved too dependent on proper wind and weather conditions to be a reliable weapon.

In September, 1916, the British produced the first tanks, throwing thirty-six of them into the Battle of the Somme. But while these new monsters impressed the soldiers who saw them and were far less vulnerable to enemy fire than the cavalry horses they replaced, they were never produced in sufficient quantity to be used effectively. Tanks, too, were new and mechanically unreliable, but there were still too many generals on both sides who did not realize that the machine gun had made cavalry obsolete, and who just did not appreciate the possibilities of the tank.

By 1917 the failures on the Western Front had brought about the dismissal of the top generals on both sides. For the Germans, an able pair who had worked well together on the Eastern Front was now in charge: Field Marshal Paul von Hindenburg, an old soldier called out of retirement after war broke out, and General Erich Ludendorff, a brilliant tactician.

For the Allies, a young and dynamic Frenchman named Robert Nivelle had taken the place of the aging Marshal Joffre as commander in chief of the French armies. The commander of the British Expeditionary Force since December, 1915, was a stubborn and unimaginative Scotsman, Sir Douglas Haig. *

*For the soldiers in the trenches—the few survivors of the slaughters of 1915-1916, and the millions of replacements—1917 did not bring many changes in their nightmare existence. They had learned to live underground much of the time in mud and water and to sleep in dugouts sometimes equipped with tables, chairs, and makeshift bunks. The dugouts were usually built strongly enough to withstand anything but a direct shell hit, but soldiers seeking protection in dugouts always ran the risk of being buried alive. They had to learn the tricks and ruses of trench warfare and simple procedures to improve the odds for survival. They learned quickly what part of their trench was dangerously exposed to enemy sniper fire; they learned to tell from the whistling sound it made if an enemy shell was going to be close, and from the sound of clippers on barbed wire that an enemy raid was coming.

During the lulls between the big offensives, small-scale raids for the purpose of securing prisoners and information were carried out by both sides, and the techniques became standard. Usually at night a raiding party with blackened faces and armed with wirecutters, grenades, and bayonets would crawl across no-man's-land to its assigned target. Or a raiding party would follow a sudden, fierce, rolling artillery barrage that would single out the target, usually a small section of enemy trench, and cut it off from help with a continuous rain of shells (a "box barrage") on its rear and each flank. In either case, whether a raid was supported by artillery or not, once the raiders reached the target they would charge with bayonets and grenades and immediately bring back as many prisoners as survived.￼

One would have thought that the murderous results of 1915-1916 had proved that frontal assaults by infantry against carefully prepared defenses could not succeed. Yet in April, 1917, three months before Pershing and his staff arrived, the new French commander, Robert Nivelle, decided to surprise the Germans with a major offensive without the usual preliminary artillery barrage.

17

This kind of surprise attack was known as the "Brusilov break-through" after its Russian originator, under whom, the year before, the Russians had lost a million men and their last hope of victory.

Unfortunately, so many people were told about Nivelle's offensive in advance—Nivelle himself was given to boasting—that the news leaked to German spies, and the German General Staff knew exactly where and when the attack was coming. The predictable result of the Second Battle of the Aisne was another defeat, with more than 350,000 French and British casualties. Many French poilus, disgusted with their generals and tired of the war, refused to obey any more orders. The mutiny was kept quiet, but more than 23,000 French soldiers were tried before courts-martial, and twenty-three ringleaders were shot.

Though they did not learn about the mutiny till later, the other shocking facts of the situation that faced the Allies in the spring of 1917, described to Pershing and his staff during their briefing in the Hotel Crillon, must have provided a sobering experience for the Yanks.

Two weeks after Pershing and his advance guard arrived in France, the first American fighting unit, fourteen thousand strong, came ashore at the French port of Saint-Nazaire. Volunteers from all over America, they had been shipped across without training in cramped transports, and many of them who stood blinking in the bright sunlight did not even know how to wear their new uniforms. Pershing arrived on the docks to inspect them as they stood at attention in their broad-brimmed campaign hats, neck-choking collars, blouses with small patch pockets, tailored breeches, and tight leggings that fitted to the calf. Their equipment included pup tents, canteens, and mess kits. Pershing looked them over with a practiced eye that quickly saw how green they were. "They are sturdy rookies," he said. "We shall make great soldiers of them."

It was Pershing's wish to hold them in the obscurity of a training area until they were ready to be seen. Instead, the French wanted the Doughboys to show the flag at once to the citizens of Paris, and Pershing could not refuse. A few days later, on July 4, a battalion of the 16th U.S. Infantry Regiment, two thirds "sturdy rookies," stood on a Paris street facing a battalion of French poilus who had been fighting a war for thirty-two months. The French soldier, bearded and warlike, wore a coat of horizon blue with swept-back skirts revealing baggy breeches and spiral gaiters. His trench helmet, also horizon blue, curved from forehead to nape of neck in a graceful arc. On the left sleeve he wore short, horizontal stripes, one for each six-month period he had spent in the zone of fire. Many Doughboys of the 16th's battalion, staring across at the poilus that July 4, 1917, would encounter such men later on, lying with their faces to the sky, the life drained from them.

Raymond Poincaré, President of the French Republic, was thinking of the exhilarating effect these Americans would have upon the weary people of France when they marched the five-mile route to Picpus Cemetery, where their commanding general would lay a wreath upon the grave of Lafayette. Pershing, on the other hand, knew that the French generals in attendance would easily detect the greenness of his troops. He knew they would be thinking, If these are American Regulars, what will the new civilian army look like? But these problems would plague only the minds of the professional soldiers. This day belonged to the Doughboys and the citizens of Paris.

Before the Doughboys began their march, Pershing visited the tomb of Napoleon, where he was offered Napoleon's sword to kiss. He strode silently among mementoes of the glories of the past and was tortured by the prospect of the future. But his embarrassment over his raw rookies was soon relieved. They began their parade, after suitable ruffles and flourishes from French trumpeters and an overture from their own regiment's brass band, and were immediately engulfed by the ecstatic French.

It mattered little whether a buck private tried to hold his unfamiliar Springfield rifle at the proper dress for right-shoulder-arms. The men of the 16th U.S. Infantry, bobbing in a sea of

French citizens, were garlanded with wreaths, flower-pelted, lip-stick-smeared, cologne-drenched. Here were the Doughboys. They were big, they were young, and there were millions more of them coming over from the richest nation on earth. "The column as it moved forward," said Pershing, "looked like a moving flower garden."

At Picpus Cemetery, before the marble tomb of Lafayette, Pershing, a man of few words, asked an old friend, Captain C. E. Stanton, who was a good speaker, to say something. While mounted police and French soldiers struggled to hold back the crowd, Captain Stanton stepped forward, saluted, and cried in French, "Lafayette, we are here!" It was a slogan that could not be improved on, and it transformed the onlookers into a weeping, shouting, laughing maelstrom.

On this magnificent note the parade ended; the glorious day was over. That night the American troops boarded trains en route to the province of Lorraine to begin the serious business of training.

Chapter

3

The Education of a Private

N O PARIS WELCOME awaited
Private Leo J. Bailey when he arrived two months later, early in
September, 1917. His company contained not a single man who
had ever fired a Springfield rifle, and few who had discharged a
firearm of any kind. Private Bailey, wearing thin barracks shoes
and canvas leggings, arrived in the village of Soulaucourt in
eastern France to begin training, his bayonet wrapped in a newspaper (few men even had scabbards), ten rounds of live ammunition in his belt, ready to beat the German to his knees. "To have
sent us to the front at that time," Bailey wrote, "would have been
murder; but we were all willing to go. We were woefully ignorant
of the basic principles of the soldier."

Soulaucourt, a village of 250 souls, was north of Chaumont,
where Pershing had set up his headquarters. In the center of the
town was a granite shaft commemorating seventeen of its sons,
dead on the field of honor. Six more lay wounded in hospitals, and
one other, home from the wars for good, hobbled around on two
sticks. These casualties, representing ten percent of the town's
total population, are a good indication of the price France had paid
in the war. Private Bailey's squad buddies astounded the villagers

when they streamed from their railroad boxcars in the chill frost of dawn, stripped to the waist, and sluiced themselves at the horse trough. If this was not an indication of madness to the French, who were said to look on soap and water with suspicion, the sight of all hands brushing teeth with horse trough water and spitting foam on the cobbles must have convinced them.

Private Bailey's company represented half of Europe. His own squad included, besides Irishman Bailey, a Jewish corporal, a Dutch immigrant named Louis Van Iersal, who was later to win the Medal of Honor, a New York Italian lad, and an immigrant from the West Indies. The company captain was an immigrant from Bohemia, and only he and the fourth platoon leader, who had been a Regular Army sergeant, knew something about soldiering. Together they set about training their men.

Bailey and his buddies had to learn the formal trench warfare of the French, with its emphasis on the Chauchat automatic rifle, a wicked light weapon of short range believed by Doughboys to have been fashioned from rusty sardine cans; on heavy Hotchkiss machine guns; on British Stokes mortars that could lob a small shell from one trench into the next; on bayonet, grenade, barbed wire, and shovel. The French paid little attention to their Lebel rifle. Little more than a musket with a three-cartridge clip, it was not very accurate, and was used mainly as a pike for a bayonet point. Frenchmen preferred to fight Germans in a clash of patrols, throwing grenades, which they carried in a bag, and resorting to the bayonet at close quarters. Neither they nor the British, who had lost most of their superb marksmen early in the war, saw much usefulness in the rifle in trench warfare.

Pershing, on the other hand, was unswerving in his insistence that raw American recruits learn to master the Springfield rifle and the techniques of open warfare. French farmers soon saw Doughboys practicing marksmanship against any hillside that was handy.

For weeks Bailey drilled in his thin-soled shoes on plowed earth, soaked by the incessant, bone-chilling rain that came early to Lorraine and the Vosges Mountains that year. For breakfast he was given a strip of bacon, two hardtack crackers, and a cup of weak coffee. At noon, after five hours of drill, the same ration was repeated with the addition of a potato boiled in its jacket. For supper, after a hard afternoon, he got a few spoonfuls of rice and another canteen cup of weak coffee.

Pershing had chosen Chaumont as General Headquarters for the AEF because it was about 150 miles east by southeast of Paris, and could be supplied by railroads from French Atlantic and Mediterranean ports that were not needed for the French and British armies. Chaumont quickly grew into a huge complex of hastily erected buildings that echoed to the clatter of typewriters and the bustle of telephone switchboards. Railway transport was vital, and Pershing brought over roundhouse hostlers, superintendents, and other experts from the States, and set about the task of supplying the huge American divisions.

Compared to the French and the British, whose divisions by 1917 had shrunk to little more than 9,000 men each, a Yank division numbered about three times that many. It consisted of two brigades of infantry, each commanded by a brigadier general, plus infantry support: two machine gun battalions, an artillery brigade, a regiment of engineers, a signal corps battalion, and a sanitary (hospital) and supply train (always called trains, though they frequently traveled by wagon or truck). The infantry units below brigade level began with a squad of eight men commanded by a corporal. Seven squads made a platoon (lieutenant), four platoons a company (captain), four companies a battalion (major), three battalions a regiment (colonel), and two regiments a brigade. Altogether a U.S. division consisted on paper of over 27,000 men, and it was usually commanded by a major general. However, due to sickness and the absence of officers and men detached to schools or to special training programs, a major general usually found himself commanding around 25,000 men. (A corps consisted of two or more divisions, and an army contained at least two corps. The Americans would not have enough divisions to form either a corps or an army until the following summer.)

Schools were started all around the Chaumont area for infantry, artillery, machine-gunners, engineers, aviators. Pershing even insisted on a school for cooks. The Iron Commander was everywhere, touring villages, climbing ladders into barn lofts, tasting the miserable slop in the cooks' kettles. Whenever he saw men dispirited or slack he issued a warning to their luckless battalion or regimental commander. He never gave an officer a second warning, and those judged unfit for command were relieved and sent to the rear. But more often he would say, "I don't see how you did it, major. But your battalion shows that you have done it. My compliments to you."

Pershing was determined that his officers learn the art of command, and that his growing army master the skills of war. Training in open warfare was relentless. As winter came the skirmishers looked like snowmen in the fields as they alternately charged and sprawled, their numb fingers working the bolts of their rifles. Drill settled down to eight hours a day, five days a week. At evening, when bugles blew Recall, troops returned to the villages and sat drenched and shivering in stables and barns on floors they had swept clean until they pleased the Iron Commander's eye. There were no campfires; men simply removed their tattered garrison shoes and rubbed numb feet with a blanket in a corner. Many barns bore such signs as: WELCOME TO VALLEY FORGE. BRING YOUR OWN POTATO.

By October 21, 1917, after three months in France, the 1st Division was judged ready to defend quiet trenches held by two French divisions in the Lunéville sector on the eastern part of the front line. It was a section of the front regarded by both sides as a rest area since each had lost 500,000 men the previous year at nearby Verdun. Unofficially, by common consent, neither side indulged in sniping. There was little machine-gun fire—usually only enough to satisfy a visiting inspector. Artillery fire was always aimed at empty fields, and raids to capture prisoners were infrequent.

The arrival of the Americans upset the peace. Every man in the Big Red One—as the division came to be known because of the red numeral on each man's shoulder patch—wanted to go on a patrol, a raid, to be the first to capture or kill a German. Sergeant Alex L. Arch, C Battery, 6th U.S. Field Artillery, fired the first round from a French 75, the most famous and universally effective artillery piece of the war, at five minutes past six of a cloudy morning, October 23. The first Doughboy wounded was 2nd Lieutenant D. H. Harden of the 26th U.S. Infantry.

Across the lines, the Germans became curious about this new activity and brought up an Assault Company of a hundred men. These were experts in the technique of raids, in the use of trench knives, Bangalore torpedoes, potato-masher grenades, Luger pistols, bayonets. When night fell on November 2 they moved into the front line. On the American side the 1st Division's 2nd Battalion, a regiment of which had marched to Lafayette's grave in July, was relieving the 1st Battalion, moving in stealthily and silently through deep, muddy communication trenches that zigzagged up to the first line. By midnight the exchange had been made. Platoon leaders earnestly inspected lines and surveyed fields of fire. Listening posts were manned. It was all new, exciting, and strange, despite the many practices in dummy trenches behind the lines.

At exactly three o'clock in the morning all hell broke loose. German artillery, mortars, and machine guns spoke in chorus, throwing tons of metal on the Yank front. After a few minutes of preparation the fire was concentrated on one sector, at first isolating in a box barrage of exploding shells on four sides F company, 2nd Battalion, 16th U.S. Infantry. Then the rain of shells isolated and cut off only one platoon of that company. The German Assault Company facing it leapt from their trenches and started across the two hundred meters separating Americans from Germans. As their Bangalore torpedoes blasted a path through the wire, the side of the box barrage nearest the Germans vanished, the other sides continuing to roar with breaking shells. The American platoon first knew of the Germans' presence when grenades burst among them.

It was over in three dark minutes of pistols, bayonets, knives.

The platoon stood its ground in the blackness and fought back. The German Assault Company left on a precise time schedule, taking its own wounded and a Doughboy sergeant and ten men. The prisoners were dragged back through the gaps in the wire, and the open side of the box barrage again was closed with forbidding shell bursts. Another three minutes and all guns ceased. Again there were only the faint noises in the dark, the sickly sweet smell of picric acid fumes, and the smoke of high explosives rolling into the trenches with the cold air of autumn dawn.

In this first American action in the war, November 3, 1917, eleven men were missing and three men lay dead in the muddy bottom of the trench: Corporal James B. Gresham, Private Thomas F. Enright, and Private Merle D. Hay. These first Americans to be killed in action were buried that afternoon in a little pasture, with a French general in attendance, and a detachment of French gunners firing a volley over their graves.

The Big Red One was relieved from front-line duty on the night of November 20, having served well in its first test under fire and having suffered few casualties. The other divisions now in France, the 2nd, 26th, and 42nd, knowing they would soon undertake such tasks, redoubled their efforts in training to make themselves into first-class fighting outfits. In the States, tens of thousands of new Doughboys were drilling with wooden guns, backed up by gunners using sawed-off telegraph poles for artillery. Others were being carried by Pullman sleepers to Atlantic ports, while people along the tracks waved and cheered. Crowded aboard transport ships, they were convoyed across the ocean by a fast-growing American Navy of cruisers and destroyers. In French ports they climbed into railroad boxcars and were carried to their assigned training areas. The French claimed the boxcars were able to hold forty men and eight horses, but somehow Americans were bigger. A common sergeant's complaint was, "I got all my forty artillerymen in the boxcar, Lieutenant. But if you try to put eight of our horses in, somebody's gonna be trampled to death." During the next twelve months 39 more American divisions would arrive in France. Six of them would be assigned to work at French ports, at Chaumont, or at American supply depots. But Doughboys in the other divisions would be put through the same rigorous training that Private Bailey and his buddies had experienced.

In Soulaucourt on Thanksgiving Day, Private Bailey and his buddies knew everything was going according to plan: every ten men of M Company had a roast turkey to share. By Christmas there were 250,000 Yanks in France, most of whom had never spent the holiday away from home before. They set about to make the best of it. Christmas meant children to these new soldiers— stockings filled with toys, trees, and colored lights. So they devoted that first Christmas to the children of France. Doughboys from one division competed with Doughboys from other divisions in providing presents and entertainment for French children, many of whom had never had so much attention or seen such generosity.

One field artillery battalion was given the village church by the local priest for its celebration. The band scheduled an afternoon parade; engineers and signalers provided a tree with lights. There was a fat Santa Claus wearing red flannel bloomers and the colonel's best boots. Santa rode a sled pulled by Hindenburg, the wagon train's gentlest mule, who was covered by a bright robe. The band led the way playing "Dixie," the battalion marched behind. Once in the church, the barbershop quartet from B Battery sang "Down in the Coal Hole," and then the presents were given out. There were capes, cloaks, mittens, real leather shoes, tin soldiers, toy battleships, dolls, fruits, candies, and nuts. Afterward there was a fireworks display using flares and rockets. It was a grand Christmas, with few lost buddies to mourn.

Across the lines, Germans in dugouts sang songs not unlike those of the Doughboys, "Silent Night" and "Tannenbaum," and received packages from home containing sweaters and chocolates. These troops, like the eager but ignorant Americans, were optimistic, and for good reason. Russia was all but out of the war. Only the month before, in November of 1917, Russia's second revolution of the year had seen the Bolsheviks, headed by Lenin and Trotsky, seize power from the provisional government which had deposed the Czar in March. Now Russia was suing for peace, and the Germans were able to start bringing their armies from the Eastern Front to France. Hindenburg and Ludendorff had drawn up careful plans for a German victory on the Western Front in 1918, and they faced the prospects of the new year with high hopes.

4

Spring, 1918:
Practice at Seicheprey and Cantigny

By MARCH, 1918, there were about 325,000 Doughboys in France, but only the 1st Division was in action. Following its first experience at Lunéville and a period of rest and more training, the Big Red One had been sent into the trenches around Seicheprey, a quiet sector of the front about 150 miles east of Paris (see map, page 43). Three other American divisions, the 26th, 2nd, and 42nd, were still in training but were almost ready. All four of them would soon be needed.

On March 21 the Germans launched their all-out offensive to end the war on the Western Front before American strength could be brought to bear. With Russia now out of the war they had moved many divisions from their Eastern Front to the west, and they planned a series of massive attacks on the British and the French. The German strategy was simple: split the Allied armies, drive the British into the sea, and then crush the French.

The German attack of March 21 caught the Allies by surprise. The blow fell on the junction of French and British armies near Saint-Quentin on the Somme River northeast of Paris, and the British Fifth Army was nearly destroyed. Exploiting their initial success, the Germans broke through British supporting lines and

29

drove west forty miles in four days to the village of Cantigny, only fifty-five miles due north of Paris. It was by far the deepest penetration by either side since 1914, and it caused heavy British and French losses (see map, page 35).

When he received the news of the German attack, Pershing set out from his headquarters at Chaumont to find Major General Ferdinand Foch, Chief of Staff of the French Army, to learn about the British situation and see what he could do. The roads were choked with transport, the air full of confusion and uncertainty. No one at French Third Army Headquarters knew where Foch was, but Pershing finally located him near Paris in a farmhouse surrounded by a cherry orchard in full bloom, a carpet of spring violets on the ground beneath.

Foch was in the kitchen with General Henri Phillipe Pétain, hero of the great French defense of the city of Verdun in 1916, and Georges Clemenceau, known as the "Tiger of France," who had become Prime Minister in November of 1917. The three of them were bent over a map stretched out on the kitchen table, debating the next move of General Erich Ludendorff, German Chief of Staff. Pershing risked offending both Clemenceau and Pétain by asking if he and Foch could speak alone. Once alone, he told Foch in his atrocious French that he would fight with "all that I have" wherever Foch wanted him to take on the veteran Germans. Pershing insisted, however, that his Yanks fight as American divisions and not be broken up as individual replacements for French and British divisions, and Foch agreed. Pershing had resolved to keep his American units together until he had built up an American Army—something he would have to fight for throughout the war. His offer showed, however, that he realized the situation was desperate.

"All that I have" meant the four divisions that Pershing believed were ready, the 1st, 26th, 2nd, and 42nd. Foch selected the 1st and the 26th, and early in April he ordered the Big Red One out of its trenches around Seicheprey and sent it to Cantigny, two hundred miles to the northwest, where the German offensive had just ground to a halt. To replace the 1st Division at Seicheprey, Foch assigned the 26th New Englanders.

The 26th was one of thirty-five National Guard divisions formed before the war's end. Each was made up of a nucleus of reservists who in peacetime spent a few weeks in training every summer. With the outbreak of war these divisions rapidly filled up their ranks as civilians volunteered for service. Under the National Defense Act of 1916, the President was permitted to draft the state guards into elements of the United States Army. When Wilson asked for war there were seventeen National Guard divisions of some 382,000 officers and men, and they would see more days of fighting than Regulars and draftees combined. These guardsmen felt they were better men than the catch-all Regulars of the peacetime Army. Officers knew all their men personally, their homes and families. There was great loyalty among them, and many of them had belonged to their division for years.

The New Englanders were in their place on a front of eleven miles around Seicheprey by April 3. The sector was on the south flank of the Saint-Mihiel salient which the Germans had held since 1914, an L-shaped protrusion into French lines that had annoyed Frenchmen for three years. It had become a comparatively quiet front, the enemy content to use it as a threat while they attacked elsewhere, but company commanders from Connecticut, Massachusetts, Maine, and Vermont were warned not to be deceived. The Germans held the high ground, and from watchtowers would order artillery to throw a salvo at anything that moved. Watching the arrival of the New Englanders, the Germans wanted to capture some prisoners and interrogate them, and they began a series of raids.

Night after night German patrols came over, outpost skirmishes sometimes lasting five days and nights. The New Englanders found this kind of hand-to-hand brawling to their liking and gave a good account of themselves, killing and capturing many Germans.

31

"How many Heinies you think came at us this morning, Sergeant?"

"Oh, not too many this morning. I'd say about three saloonsful."

Nettled at being bested in so many stand-up-and-fight encounters, on April 10 the Germans came over behind a barrage with some eight hundred men. There was fierce fighting for two days, and there were many feats of reckless bravery on both sides. When American artillery failed to support a counterattack, Sergeant John A. Dickerson and his squad, with two Stokes mortars, stuck to their exposed position and gave all the support their little guns could supply. Three of Dickerson's privates were killed, one wounded, and Dickerson himself, having lost an eye and a leg, continued to give advice to a surviving private and corporal working the guns.

The Germans had suffered three-to-one casualties in these engagements and they were growing angry. They brought up their elite assault troops, studied Yankee troop dispositions, and began rehearsing for a big raid. Nothing was left to chance. German scouts in Doughboy uniforms infiltrated behind American lines and picked up all kinds of information, some of it from a captured mail sack. They knew their artillery had driven the 26th's ablest brigade commander, Peter E. Traub, from his headquarters, and they knew the names of various Doughboy company cooks.

Around three in the morning of April 20 a heavy German artillery barrage opened up. As it rolled forward over American positions it was followed by a force of 3,200 Germans, their assignment to capture and hold Seicheprey, other villages along the line, and the woods on the Doughboys' right.

The German raid proceeded with smashing success. Seicheprey was pinched on both flanks, the four hundred Doughboys in the town apparently doomed. The Yankee lines here had been badly mangled in the horrendous bombardment, one platoon reduced from fifty to eight men before attackers ever reached them. The Germans surrounded the town, moved into the streets to clean out cellars and gun pits, clubbed machine gunners and infantry-men with rifles, and captured a Yank surgeon. German veterans began to unsling their heavy packs and consolidate their hold on the village.

The raiders had reached their first targets around 5:05 A.M. But by the time a wounded Doughboy runner staggered into Regimental Headquarters at six-thirty to report the shocking news that Seicheprey was in enemy hands, a counterattack had already started. Remnants of Major George A. Rau's shattered Connecti-cut battalion, caught earlier in a box barrage, drove the Germans from the village and held on with what they had left. Rau's force was made up of orderlies, clerks, runners, kitchen helpers—the cook went along with a cleaver and was seen to split a German skull before he died—and a detachment of twenty-five Doughboys from the 1st Division who had misbehaved and been left behind to clean up the area as a disciplinary measure.

The Germans had even tougher going in the woods to the right of the village. Desperate man-to-man fighting continued all day among the rocks and trees, a situation in which the tactical skill of the veteran assault troops counted for little. The Ger-mans had lost their advantage after the first shock and now faced New England boys who had no intention of giving up the woods. Without reinforcements they drove the Germans out, even re-capturing the difficult trench beyond.

In the aftermath the woods was a picture each American sur-vivor would long remember: a dead Yank machine gunner and his helper slumped by their gun, the gunner's hands still on the gun's handles, the helper frozen in the attitude of feeding a strip of D.M. cartridges into the guides—both killed in action by two Germans who also now lay dead before them.

The Germans withdrew, taking 136 American prisoners, leav-ing behind 60 percent of two Doughboy Infantry companies and one machine-gun company killed or wounded. They admitted a total of six hundred casualties and left behind 160 German dead and one hundred prisoners. Still, they claimed a victory over the ignorant Americans, and turned it to propaganda uses.

The Yankees thought otherwise. Green troops, they had been placed in difficult positions to be held at all costs, had been savagely molested, and had recovered these positions against the cream of German assault troops. Their morale was sky high.

Back home Seicheprey was hailed as a great victory, the news coming just in time to stimulate the civilian war effort by bolstering sales for the Third Liberty Loan. Patriotic citizens rushed to buy Government War Bonds to help finance the tremendous cost of the war. The New Englanders stayed on in this "quiet" sector into June, suffering 2,891 casualties as they became battle-tested. Seicheprey was the first engagement of Doughboys in any sizable force, and it was a picture in miniature of what would happen to a million of their buddies in 1918.

While the New Englanders were getting a taste of defensive warfare at Seicheprey, the German main effort had shifted from the Somme River front to Flanders, far to the northwest. There the Germans struck the British a nearly fatal smash in April and caused further heavy British losses. This second blow in the German offensive was not as successful as the first in terms of miles gained, but it had the French and British armies in desperate straits.

The arrival of the Doughboys of the Big Red One at Cantigny during the last week of April was a tonic to the French. The 1st Division's orders were to reinforce the exhausted French First Army, which had rushed to the support of the British Fifth Army and had barely succeeded in stopping the first movement of the great German offensive on the Somme after a forty-mile advance. When the Doughboys arrived at Cantigny and went into the line, the Germans, through their intelligence sources, knew it. Whenever an American division appeared, the Germans were under orders to hit it particularly hard in the hope of damaging American morale. They wasted little time in testing the Doughboys of the Big Red One. On the night of May 3 a massive barrage with both high explosive and gas shells caused eight hundred casualties. For the next ten nights German batteries raked

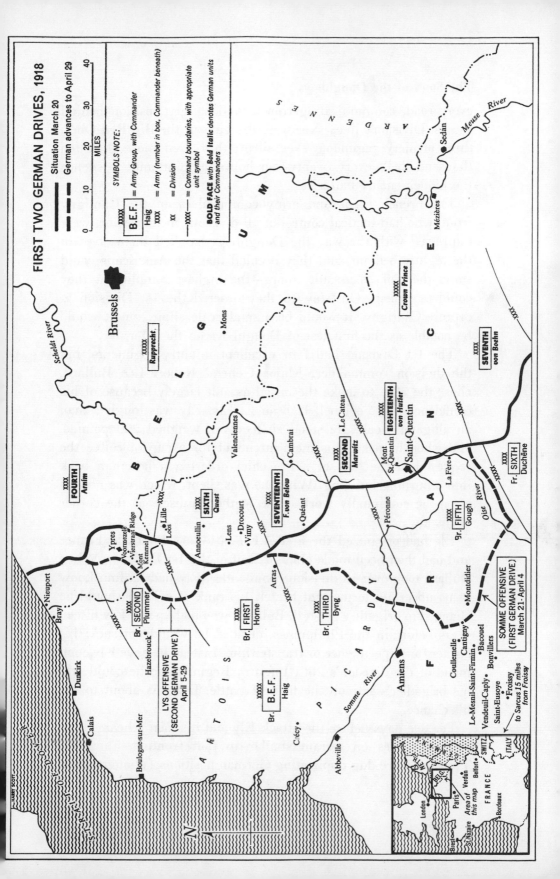

FIRST TWO GERMAN DRIVES, 1918

━━━ Situation March 20
╺╺╺╺ German advances to April 29

MILES
0   10   20   30   40

SYMBOLS NOTE:

B.E.F.	= Army Group, with Commander
Haig	
xxxx	= Army (number in box, Commander beneath)
xx	= Division
xxxx	= Command boundaries, with appropriate unit symbol

BOLD FACE with **Bold Italic** denotes German units and their Commanders

Scheldt River

Brussels

B E L G I U M

•Mons

xxxxx
Rupprecht

Meuse River

•Sédan

A R D E N N E S

•Mézières

xxxx
SEVENTH
von Boehn

Crown Prince

xxxx
FOURTH
Arnim

Valenciennes•

•Cambrai

•Le Cateau

xxxx
SECOND
Marwitz

Mont
St-Quentin•
Saint-Quentin

xxxx
EIGHTEENTH
von Hutier

xxxx
SIXTH
Quast

•Lille
•Loos
Annoeullin•

•Lens
•Vimy
•Drocourt

•Quéant

xxxx
SEVENTEENTH
F. von Below

P I C A R D Y

•Péronne

La Fère•

Oise River

Fr. SIXTH
Duchêne

Nieuport•
•Ypres
•Voormezeele
Vierstraat Ridge
Mont Kemmel

xxxx
Br. SECOND
Plumer

Brày•
Dunkirk■

xxxx
Br. FIRST
Horne

Hazebrouck•

•Arras

xxxx
Br. THIRD
Byng

LYS OFFENSIVE
(SECOND GERMAN DRIVE)
April 5–29

A R T O I S

Calais■

Boulogne-sur-Mer•

xxxxx
B.E.F.
Haig

Somme River

Amiens■

Crécy•

Abbeville■

•Coullemelle
•Cantigny
Le-Mesnil-Saint-Firmin•
Vendeuil-Caply• •Bacouel
•Bonvillers
Saint-Eusoye•
•Froissy
•Montdidier

to Sarcus 15 mi/es
from Froissy

xxxx
FIFTH
Gough

SOMME OFFENSIVE
(FIRST GERMAN DRIVE)
March 21–April 4

F R A N C E

N

HARRY SCOTT

London•

BELG.

Brest•
St. Nazaire•

Paris• •Verdun
•Sédan

FRANCE

Belfort• SWITZ.

Bordeaux•

ITALY

Area of
this map

every road, communicating trench, and battery position behind the 1st Division's lines. Nor were the guns of the Big Red One's three artillery regiments ever silent; they fired more than ten thousand shells every twenty-four hours in an attempt to silence the hidden enemy batteries.

The French corps and army commanders on the Cantigny front, who had tactical control of all divisions in the sector, were impressed with the way the Doughboys handled themselves in the nightly bedlam, and they decided that the Americans could stand the gaff as assault troops—the highest compliment they could pay them. On May 15 they ordered the 1st Division to capture Cantigny. It would be a small-scale affair, but it would be notable as the first test of Doughboys on the offensive.

The 1st Division had four excellent infantry regiments, but the division commander, Major General Robert Lee Bullard, chose the 28th to make the initial assault largely because of his confidence in its colonel, Hanson E. Ely. Ely was tougher than an alligator steak. He stood six-feet-two, weighed 220 pounds, and when he asked his mess attendant for a cup of coffee the request had the tone of a fire chief ordering a hoseman back into a burning building. When he was silent, which was not too often, he continually worked the leathery muscle at the corner of his jaw.

Ely had organized the first A.E.F. Military Police in France and had then been made chief of staff of the 1st Division. When Bullard took over as division commander, Ely had let him know in no uncertain terms that he felt his rank of colonel should be changed to brigadier general. Bullard, who had known Ely fifteen years before in the Philippines, decided he would not sack this fighter for impertinence or transfer him. Instead he gave Ely command of the division's 28th Infantry Regiment so he could win his brigadier's star on the field of battle. Ely was about to get his chance.

For five days before the attack Ely and his men rehearsed behind the lines on terrain similar to that fronting Cantigny. Trenches were dug duplicating German positions (photographed by French observation planes) and every phase of the operation, including the evacuation of wounded, was gone over in detail.

The Germans had their own aerial reconnaissance, and their observers could tell something was up. They stepped up their shelling, and they decided to try to capture some prisoners in a raid planned for the early morning of May 27, one day before the Big Red One had scheduled its attack. After an hour and a half of heavy shelling, two raiding parties with the code names *Tarnapol* and *Tannenberg* (recalling German victories against Russia) came over. The Tannenberg raiders were annihilated before they reached Doughboy lines, but the Tarnapol group reached the first trench and was driven out only after severe fighting. One stunned Doughboy, being dragged back to German lines, was rescued by his buddies who pursued and bayonetted his captors. The 28th Infantry suffered thirty-three casualties in the raid, but the Germans captured no prisoners and gained no information.

The morning of May 28 came early, with a light haze upon the ground between the lines. At 4:45 American artillery began tuning up, checking the range and making adjustments, and thirty minutes later the guns were firing with such furious cadence that no Doughboy in the assault wave could hear the commands. Platoon leaders moved along the jump-off trenches, checking equipment, while their sleepless men blew sand from cartridge clips and fastened bayonets to the studs on their rifles. There was no elation now, only swift pulses and dedication. Some lads opened khaki-backed Bibles and turned to the Ninety-first Psalm: "A thousand shall fall at thy side, and ten thousand at thy right hand; but it shall not come nigh thee."

At 6:45, after ninety minutes of shelling by the thundering guns, a rolling barrage began exploding one hundred yards beyond the front-line trenches. This was the signal. Doughboy infantrymen, burdened under heavy packs, each man's shovel protruding above his left shoulder, struggled "over the top" and began walking across the fields toward Cantigny, following the protective curtain of fire for a distance of about ten city blocks. It all went like clockwork, with few casualties; by 7:20 the town was captured, and all objectives were reached. The second wave strung barbed wire; signalers and engineers ran telephone lines to Colonel Ely's new command post and then to battalion commanders. Out beyond Cantigny, many Doughboys set to work with their shovels strengthening captured German trenches. For a short time American artillery enclosed the area in a protective box barrage.

The real test for Ely and his men would be to hold the position against the German pros. As the sun rose higher in the sky, the Doughboys braced themselves for a counterattack. It did not materialize during the morning, but German artillery fire, aided by the aerial spotting of a flight of their famous Fokker airplanes, began to register with murderous effect on the new American positions. At two-thirty in the afternoon Ely received the unwelcome news that he was going to be attacked, probably where his right flank joined the left flank of the 26th Infantry. This estimate of German intentions had been made by Lieutenant Colonel George C. Marshall, Jr., who had succeeded Ely as division chief of staff. Some twenty years later Marshall would be supreme U.S. military commander in World War. II.

Around five-thirty in the afternoon the German attack began. Following a barrage of heavy mortars, thin waves of German Bangalore torpedo-men came into the open to blast holes in the newly erected barbed wire. Ely's front-line infantry, standing upright under the mortar fire, shot them down. A few minutes later, the first wave of German infantry stepped out following a rolling barrage of light mortars. Only a few reached the Doughboy forward trenches before they were killed or surrendered, crying "*Kamerad!*" The second and third waves fared worse than the first as American artillery, once alerted, found the range with devastating accuracy. The new American positions were too strong to be taken without the aid of massive artillery support.

Profiting from their mistake, the Germans began to plaster the Doughboys with heavy shellfire during the night. Soon the front line was no longer a line but a series of shell holes, where wounded lay with first-aid bandages stiffening in the night air, mouths cottony with bloody spittle, their bodies shuddering with pain as shock diminished. Ely called for extra stretcher bearers and field medics—his own being now among the wounded—to get these men out, and then reported to his brigadier: "Two officers left in one battalion. All men in one company gone but twelve. He will stay but should be allowed to reinforce." Who was "He," with his eleven men, who sent word to Ely he would stay? "He" remains nameless, just a Doughboy, new to war, some three thousand miles from home. Bullard immediately ordered relief of the shattered company. Meanwhile the division machine-gun officer reported: "Line in front of Cantigny probably lost. Our troops to counterattack when barrage starts."

Under cover of darkness the field medics, carriers, and ambulance men Ely had called for felt their way into the shambles of the front line. It was the roughest of assignments, but there were no men in the A.E.F. who were better trained for their specialty. Their chief was Colonel James Irving Mabee, an old Regular who had served in the Philippines, and he gave his men no easy time. "There is no maybe about Mabee" was their stock pun.

Mabee had set up his three field hospitals at the best sites he could find along the single shell-marked road leading out of Cantigny. To get into the town and up to the front lines, ambulance drivers moved their sprightly Model-T Fords or General Motors heavier rigs along the main road, having to turn out for ammunition trains—always a priority for men under fire—and then drove hell-for-leather up a ravine, dodging shell holes and skirting craters. The entire trip had to be made in darkness, except for the star shells and Very pistol flares that occasionally seared the night sky. Yet many trips were made before dawn, bringing out lads with broken bones and shrapnel wounds to waiting American Army surgeons and nurses.

On the morning of the 29th, German artillery began sending Ely everything they had in the way of high explosive and toxic

39

shells. Hoping he had been weakened, German infantry went after him three times in the afternoon. Ely managed to drive them back each time. Around suppertime Ely sent word to Bullard: "Front line pounded to hell-and-gone, and entire front line must be relieved tomorrow night or I will not be held responsible." The second night descended, bringing with it darkness, confusion, and uncertainty.

In the small hours of May 29–30, after another attack by German infantry had been repulsed, Bullard ordered Ely and the 28th out of the lines. So the following night, May 30–31, while the 16th Infantry moved in under fire to replace them, Ely and the remnants of the 28th marched back to villages miles behind the lines. The regiment had attacked the morning of May 28 with 122 officers and 3,757 men. Three days later the regimental adjutant, counting the survivors sprawling exhausted around three small French villages, reported 187 killed and 636 wounded. These losses would seem small in the days ahead.

The German commanders blamed the failures of their counterattacks at Cantigny on poor timing and organization. They were worried that "the influence of the recent operation" would have a bad effect on their men, and they agreed that the Doughboys would have to be taught a lesson or there was no telling where the thing might end.

Back home the newspapers broke out banner headlines to announce an American "first," the capture of Cantigny, though censorship permitted no mention of the Big Red One. In London, Prime Minister Lloyd George made brief mention of Cantigny as a bright patch in an otherwise melancholy sky. Ferdinand Foch had no time to praise the Americans. He had been appointed to a new position of commander in chief of all Allied forces following the success of the German offensive launched in March. At the time of the Cantigny attack he was occupied with a desperate situation sixty miles to the southeast at Château-Thierry on the Marne.

Chapter

5

Plugging the Château-Thierry Gap

T̲H̲E̲ ̲G̲E̲R̲M̲A̲N̲ Chief of Staff, General Erich Ludendorff, was pleased with the results of his March attack that had driven all the way to Cantigny, and with his April smash against the British in Flanders. But while he had inflicted heavy losses on the Allies and captured some additional French territory, he had not yet succeeded in separating the French and British armies or in driving the British into the sea. To achieve the desired split of allied forces he planned a third attack further east, counting on Foch to pull his reserves away from the juncture of French and British lines to defend against this new threat. If this third attack succeeded, Ludendorff planned a fourth attack at the weakened joint that he hoped would result in the capture of Paris.

The site of Ludendorff's third offensive of the spring of 1918 was suggested by German Intelligence, whose agents discovered that Major General Duchêne, commanding the French Sixth Army north of the Aisne River, had crowded his forward lines with troops where an important road, the *Chemin des Dames* (Road of the Ladies), ran along a vulnerable ridge. Ludendorff's agents also learned that the area behind the French front lines, which should have been bristling with pillboxes, guns, and tanks, was only lightly held. It was a situation made to order for Ludendorff's tactical genius, and he made the most of it.

Before dawn on May 27, the day before the 1st Division's small-scale attack at Cantigny, Ludendorff sent General Max von Boehn's Seventh Army, three hundred thousand men strong, smashing south against the French line on the Chemin des Dames. The assault had been prepared in secrecy and came as a great surprise. As the German army had moved up, axle boxes on caissons and wagons were muffled against clacking, horses hooves were bagged with gunny sacking, and harness buckles were greased to prevent their jingling or glinting. German infantry had moved forward along side roads in darkness, lying hidden in forests during the day to avoid detection from French reconnaissance planes.

Within hours after the first German gun spoke, whole French divisions ceased to exist. Many poilu prisoners were led back to German cages with brains so scrambled from concussion caused by the sudden, horrendous shelling that they never regained sanity. The swarm of German professionals swept forward on a thirty-mile front, gobbling up Soissons and its great railway yards on the west flank and threatening the historic cathedral city of Reims on the east flank. They seized airplanes, shops, stores, 650 guns, 2,000 machine guns, and 60,000 prisoners and headed for the Marne River thirty miles due south.

As can be seen on the map, the Marne flows west to Château-Thierry, which lies on both sides of the river some fifty miles northeast of Paris, and then turns abruptly south. East of Château-Thierry the river formed a natural defensive line which the Germans would have to cross by boat under fire, for surely the French would blow up the bridges. West of the town, however, there was no natural barrier. Foch's problem, then, was threefold: to make sure the river line was held from Château-Thierry east; to plug the gap to the west; and, despite his tremendous losses, to find the troops to do the job.

Pershing went to see Sir Douglas Haig, commander of all

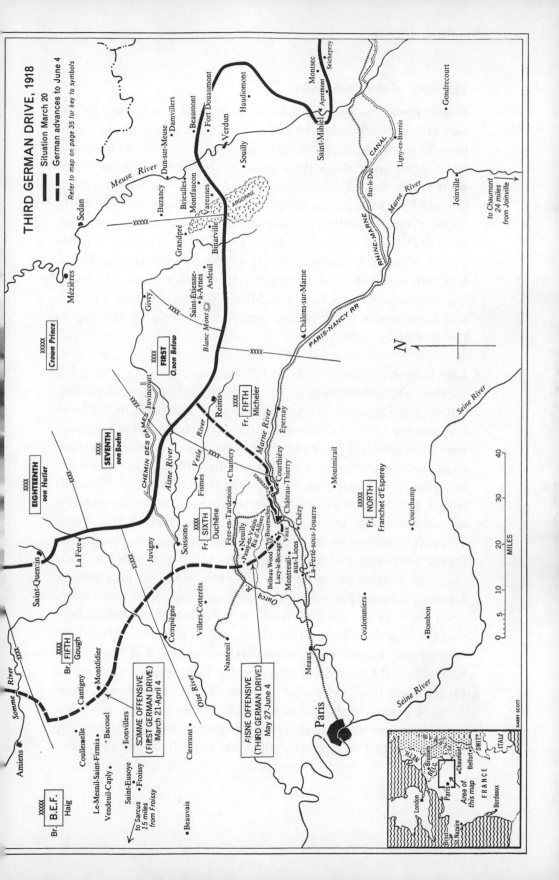

THIRD GERMAN DRIVE, 1918

Situation March 20
German advances to June 4

Refer to map on page 35 for key to symbols

N

MILES
0   5   10   20   30   40

Amiens

Somme River

XXXXX
Br. B.E.F.
Haig

Coullemelle
Le-Mesnil-Saint-Firmin
Vendeuil-Caply
Saint-Eusoye
Froissy

to Sarcus
15 miles
from Froissy

Beauvais

XXXX
Br. FIFTH
Gough

Cantigny
Montdidier
Bacouel
Fonvillers

Clermont

Oise River

Compiègne

Villers-Cotterêts

Nanteuil

Meaux

Paris

Seine River

Coulommiers

Bombon

SOMME OFFENSIVE
(FIRST GERMAN DRIVE)
March 21-April 4

AISNE OFFENSIVE
(THIRD GERMAN DRIVE)
May 27-June 4

XXXX
EIGHTEENTH
von Hutier

Saint-Quentin

La Fère

Juvigny

Soissons

Fère-en-Tardenois
Neuilly
Passy-en-Valois
Ru d'Allan
Belleau Wood
Lucy-le-Bocage
Montreuil-
aux-Lions

XXXX
SEVENTH
von Boehm

CHEMIN DES DAMES

Aisne River

Fismes
Vesle River

Chamery

XXXX
Fr. SIXTH
Duchêne

Boureschs
Vaux
Château-Thierry
Chézy

La-Ferté-sous-Jouarre

XXXXX
Fr. NORTH
Franchet d'Esperey

Courchamp

Montmirail

Juvincourt

XXXX
Crown Prince

XXXX
FIRST
O. von Below

Blanc Mont

Reims
XXXX
Fr. FIFTH
Micheler

Marne River

Courthiézy
Epernay

RHINE-MARNE

Châlons-sur-Marne

PARIS-NANCY RR

Sedan

Mézières

Meuse River

Dun-sur-Meuse
Buzancy
Brieulles
Montfaucon
Varennes
Binarville

ARGONNE

Grandpré

Givry
Saint-Étienne-
à-Arnes
Ardeuil

Damvillers
Beaumont
Fort Douaumont
Verdun
Souilly
Haudimont

Saint-Mihiel

Montsec
Apremont
Seicheprey

Gondrecourt

Joinville

Ligny-en-Barrois
Bar-le-Duc

CANAL

to Chaumont
24 miles
from Joinville

Marne River

Seine River

HARRY SCOTT

NETH.
Brussels
B.E.G.
London
Paris
Chaumont
SWITZ.
Belfort
FRANCE
ITALY
Brest
St. Nazaire
Bordeaux
Area of
this map

British forces, as soon as possible after the German assault began, arriving for breakfast on May 30. There were several Doughboy divisions training in the British sector, and Pershing immediately went about the area inspecting them. That night he went to dine with Foch at Sarcus, and, before leaving, Pershing granted Foch's request to bring his five green divisions—the 35th, 82nd, 77th, and 28th (all four divisions National Guard) and the 4th Regulars—into the Marne area. He also agreed to order up the seventen thousand infantry of the 3rd Division of Regulars (whose artillery and engineers were still scattered in training and unready) to hold the Marne line at Château-Thierry, and to make the 2nd Division available to help plug the gap to the west of the town.

Late in the afternoon of May 31, Lieutenant John T. Bissell led fourteen Doughboys of the 7th (motorized) Machine-Gun Battalion, 3rd Division, across the wagon bridge over the Marne and into the town of Château-Thierry. The first of the American reinforcements, they carried with them two Hotchkiss machine guns, and their mission was to cover the retreat of the remnants of a French Colonial division of Senegalese—magnificent assault troops. While Bissell and his men set up their two guns to cover approaches to the bridge, other elements of their battalion dug gun emplacements on the south side of the Marne. In spite of frantic confusion and haste, by midnight all the American machine guns were emplaced, the Doughboys having dug two alternate positions for each gun, with a fourth kept secret and known only to platoon leaders. (It was discovered six weeks later that German spies knew about these secret positions.) From time to time the diggers dropped their shovels and fired streams of bullets into the town square across the river, taking care not to hit the retreating Senegalese. By ten o'clock the next day, June 1, the Germans had reached the river's edge, driving what remained of the Senegalese onto the wagon bridge. When the fighting reached the middle of the span, French demolition teams,

44

having placed all their charges, blew up the bridge, sending attackers and defenders into eternity with the same breath of fire. No one knew for two days if Bissell and his fourteen buddies had been on the bridge.

During the next twenty-four hours the 3rd Division's seventeen thousand infantrymen filtered in and prepared defensive lines on the south side of the river. There was sniping and cannonading, and there were many aerial dogfights overhead. At Jaulgonne, six miles east of Château-Thierry, Germans tried to slip across the Marne but were driven back by poilus and Doughboys. On the night of June 2, Lieutenant E. W. Cobbey, 2nd, thought he heard someone calling him from across the river. Taking the chance it was not a German ruse, he crawled over the ties of the railway bridge and brought back his friend Lieutenant Bissell and thirteen of Bissell's men. One man and both Hotchkiss guns were missing. Another lieutenant, W. R. Flannery, hearing some cries from the north bank, swam across the river with his Colt .45 lashed on top of his head and brought back a wounded Frenchman.

The 2nd Division, made up of twin brigades of Regulars and Marines, had been alerted on May 29 to relieve the Big Red One at Cantigny, but in answer to the new emergency the division was ordered on May 30 to move by truck at five the next morning to the Paris-Meaux area in the direction of Château-Thierry.

Before dawn on the 31st, Private Bailey, Chauchat gunner of the 9th Infantry Regiment, marched several miles and then was crowded with nineteen buddies into the stake body of a small blue truck. He had no knowledge of his destination. He only knew that the French had been defeated north of Château-Thierry and the division's orders had been changed. The long line of trucks set off on roads that were soon shrouded in dust that covered the olive-drab uniforms of the Doughboys with a mantle of gray chalk. Around noon there was a halt, and each man ate a salty bacon sandwich. Near dusk the trucks rumbled through the de-

45

serted town of Meaux and swung up the road toward Château-Thierry, and for the first time Bailey began to see civilian refugees in flight.

"One who saw that stream of misery can never forget it," he wrote.

> There were people of all ages except military ages; there were children riding on creaking wagons, held in place by their feeble grandparents; everyone who was able to do so was compelled to walk. There were carts drawn by every conceivable animal: cows, oxen, dogs, and horses. The other cattle were driven along by the side of the wagons. The procession was noiseless, for the marchers were too miserable to more than glance at us as we passed and probably thought: *A few more for the Boches to devour*. Alongside the road, too tired to go farther, was a leathery-faced old woman with all her remaining property piled on a wheelbarrow . . . each procession occupied half of the hot, white road from which there arose a cloud of bitter dust—the young going up to slaughter and be slaughtered; the old and their youth fleeing from the *furor Teutonicus*. Each half pitied the other, and the fresher half swore to avenge the feebler.

That night Bailey and his squad left the trucks and marched forward, burdened under two Chauchats, ammunition clips, Springfield rifles and bandoliers, heavy packs, field rations, and two hundred pistol rounds. At midnight they stretched out on the cobblestones of a deserted town square and slept the sleep of exhaustion. At dawn remnants of French regiments streamed through the town heading for the rear. "Many of the men told us we would never stop the Boches," Bailey recalled. Soon the Doughboys were marching on through the heat of the summer day and passing more disheartened and retreating Frenchmen. By noon there were no more retreating infantry, only a few forlorn artillerymen firing siege guns at woods and fields beyond. The Germans were ahead and coming on, but no one knew exactly where they were.

The confusion was excusable since there was no front; there were only roads choked with refugees, troops, and limousines of staff officers—all in retreat. The French staff issued three different sets of battle orders to the 2nd Division in rapid succession. Cynical Marines on the staff of Brigadier General James G. Harbord, commanding the Marine Brigade of the 2nd Division, advised him that when it came to French battle orders, "a good Marine never goes into motion until he gets the third edition." Harbord, an ex-enlisted man in the Regular Army, had been Pershing's chief of staff at Chaumont. When Pershing gave Harbord the Marine Brigade he said it was the best in France and if Harbord failed he would know whom to blame. Already Harbord's men had begun to look on him as "a good Marine," and in the eyes of the Corps nobody since 1775 had ever been better than a good Marine.

Like Bailey and his buddies of the Doughboy Brigade, Harbord and his Marines had come up the road from Paris by truck and then on foot. On the night of June 1 Harbord set up headquarters in the village of Lucy-le-Bocage, where French General Michel's retreating personnel were busily looting, ripping open parlor sofas in search of hoarded gold, throwing furniture from windows, stuffing their knapsacks with laces and linens, and battering in the doors of wine cellars. (If *they* didn't loot the town the Germans would.) Just ahead lay a small forest whose name, Belleau Wood, would soon become famous. There General Michel, commanding this sector, still hoped he had some troops fighting. Michel proposed an immediate counterattack together with the Marines, but wiser American heads prevailed. "The proper way to stop an advance is to form a line and hold it," said Colonel Preston Brown, 2nd Division chief of staff. A gloomier Frenchman advised Colonel Wendell C. Neville, commanding the 5th Marine Regiment, that the best thing to do was retreat. Neville, an Annapolis graduate who wore the Medal of Honor, replied, "Retreat, hell. We just got here."

Somehow during the confusion of the night a line was formed, the 6th and 5th Marine Regiments in the center, the 23rd Regiment of Doughboys on the left flank and the 9th on the right. Everyone hoped that somewhere to the right of the 9th the rem-

47

nants of the French Senegalese who had escaped Château-Thierry would form a flank hard by the town, with the U.S. 3rd Division just across the Marne. What force would hold on the left flank of the 23rd Regiment was uncertain. But any doubts about the whereabouts of the Germans was quickly dispelled. At dawn on June 2 fierce German elements attacked the 23rd Infantry on the left, and other Germans struck the Marine center. They were just as fiercely beaten back, and an historic fight was on.

Chapter

6

Belleau Wood

On the morning of June 3, General Michel informed the 2nd Division that he had lost Belleau Wood during the night. The news did not greatly perturb Michel's corps commander, Major General Jean Degoutte, who would soon prove to have little regard for the lives of the men in his command, whether French or American. Degoutte had every intention of retaking the wood with the brawny Doughboys and Marines.

During June 4 and 5 the Americans beat off exploratory attacks by the Germans and improved their lines, the 23rd Infantry side-slipping east to join the 9th, the two Marine regiments in turn inching westward. On the night of the 5th, Degoutte passed the word that the Marines would counterattack at dawn the next morning, their objective Belleau Wood. It would be a blind attack, for he did not know enemy strength or disposition there, and it would take place without the support of mortars or hand grenades, or the advantage of careful rehearsals. The first movement would be to seize positions in patches of trees and on hillocks facing the wheat fields that stretched north to Belleau Wood. After attaining this position the Marines would then, at

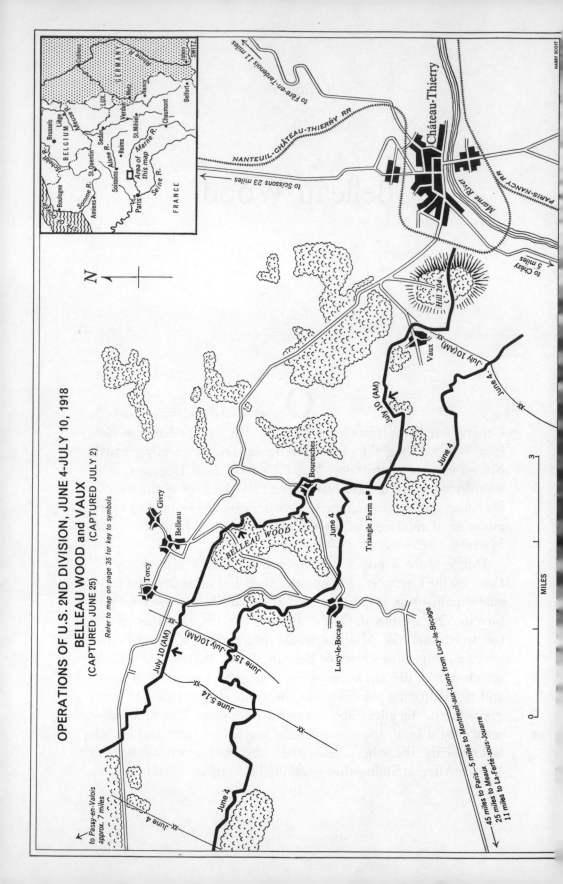

OPERATIONS OF U.S. 2ND DIVISION, JUNE 4–JULY 10, 1918
BELLEAU WOOD and VAUX
(CAPTURED JUNE 25) (CAPTURED JULY 2)

Refer to map on page 35 for key to symbols

N

HARRY SCOTT

Château-Thierry

Hill 204

BELLEAU WOOD

Belleau

Givry

Torcy

Bouresches

Triangle Farm

Lucy-le-Bocage

Vaux

Marne River

NANTEUIL-CHÂTEAU-THIERRY RR

PARIS-NANCY RR

to Scissons 23 miles

to Fère-en-Tardenois 11 miles

to Chézy 5 miles

to Passy-en-Valois approx. 7 miles

45 miles to Paris—5 miles to Montreuil-aux-Lions from Lucy-le-Bocage
25 miles to Meaux
11 miles to La-Ferté-sous-Jouarre

June 4

June 5–14

June 15–July 10 (AM)

July 10 (AM)

July 10 (AM)

MILES
0   1   2   3

Area of this map

GERMANY
BELGIUM
FRANCE
LUX.
SWITZ.
Rhine R.
Meuse R.
Moselle R.
Scheldt R.
Somme R.
Aisne R.
Marne R.
Seine R.
Coblenz
Brussels
Liège
Sedan
St. Quentin
Amiens
Boulogne
Verdun
Metz
Nancy
Belfort
Chaumont
St. Mihiel
Reims
Soissons
Paris

5 P.M., cross the wheat fields to seize the wood. The 23rd and 9th Infantry were ordered to support the Marines on the right flank with heavy fire, but not to charge.

Led by lieutenants in Sam Browne belts—prime targets for machine gunners and telescopic riflemen—and armed with rifles and bayonets, Chauchats and Hotchkiss machine guns, the first wave of Marines stepped out on schedule on June 6. The movement went off with dash and verve, but it was rough all along the line, with furious fighting and bayonet work until noon. Messages told the story: "We have reached our objective and are entrenching," reported Major Julius Turril. "Williams is up on the left with three platoons—Hamilton in the center and Winans on the right—the remnants of other companies have joined the other two." And the chief liaison officer from Pershing's headquarters, Major Roberts, informed Chaumont the operation was "an entire success."

The first part of the day's attack having succeeded, Degoutte informed Harbord shortly after noon to carry out the second step, the assault on Belleau Wood at 5 P.M. As seen from the air the wood looked like a sea horse, its head and curling tail facing west. Above its head was the town of Belleau, German command post; just to the southeast was the disputed village of Bouresches. The Marines would also have to take and hold Bouresches, for if the Germans held on to the village they could pour murderous fire from its walled gardens and stone houses into the right flank of the Marines in Belleau Wood. At this moment, and unknown to anyone but the Germans, the wood concealed two German battalions with thirty-two light and sixteen heavy machine guns, plus reserve support. Machine gunners were spread out behind huge boulders in small ravines, hidden in the second-growth timber and the mass of brush that carpeted the ground.

Private Bailey was a witness to what happened next. All day he and his buddies of the 9th Infantry had lain in support of the Marines near Lucy-le-Bocage south of the wood, listening to "the hellish chatter and roaring of our guns." He wrote:

For the last few minutes before five the fire was terrible. At exactly five there was a silence . . . then the guns were directed to the fields behind Belleau Wood to prevent the Germans from bringing up reinforcements. . . . We saw the long lines of Marines leap from somewhere and start across the wheatfields toward the woods. Those lines were straight and moved steadily, a few paces in front of each its officer leading, not driving. The attackers went up the gentle slope and, as the first wave disappeared over the crest we heard the opening clatter of dozens of machine guns that sprayed the advancing lines. Then we heard some shrieks that made our blood run cold. High above the roar of the artillery and the clatter of machine guns we heard the war cries of the Marines. The lines continued to go over the crest and, as the last disappeared, we began to notice that a machine gun would go out of action. This meant that the Marines were either shooting the gunners or crawling up and bayoneting the crews. . . . How long this took I do not know, but it seemed less than half an hour before all the machine guns had stopped firing. . . . Directly in front of us, though concealed by some woods, the Marines had attacked and captured Bouresches.

As night fell on June 6, messages began to filter back. "What is left of the battalion is in woods close by. Do not know whether will be able to stand or not." "Unable to advance farther. . . . Losses already heavy." No one really knew the full story, but the Marines had paid a fearful price and were in possession of only a portion of the wood. It had been the hardest day in American military history since the Civil War, yet it was only a foretaste of the terrible days ahead.

That night the Marine survivors lay exhausted in the confused tangle of the wood, uncertain of their ability to drive back the German counterattack that would surely come. The next day, June 7, they strengthened their lines, tended the wounded, brought up food and ammunition, and tried unsuccessfully to locate German strongpoints. Fortunately the German attack did not come until June 8, and with the help of reinforcements was driven back. For the next six days fighting raged back and forth in a complete stalemate, with each side sending up reinforcements in driblets. In their charge on June 6 the Marines had captured the town of Bouresches in a fierce house-to-house struggle, but the Germans were able to pour such deadly fire into it from the surrounding woods that it was almost impossible to hold or support it. On the 13th Harbord received word that the enemy had taken Bouresches, and he ordered two companies out of reserve for a dawn counterattack to recapture the town. Eight minutes later he canceled the order. "I have a message, received at 5:25 from my major in Bouresches that we still hold it," he explained.

By this time Harbord's Marine Brigade had been fighting thirteen days without relief, not a man having taken off his shoes, few having received a cup of hot coffee. It was the practice of the British and French to have their battalions leapfrog forward over one another in turn, and never to subject one outfit to more than four or five days of continuous attack. Harbord called this to the attention of his superiors and demanded that his men be relieved. The problem was to find an outfit that was available— not an easy task in the emergency. The lot fell to the 7th Infantry Regiment of the 3rd Division, undergoing training south of Château-Thierry. On the night of June 16, while Marines were still exchanging fire with German machine gunners, Doughboys of the 7th Infantry began moving into the scattered foxholes of Belleau Wood.

The exhausted Marines, one battalion minus sixty-four percent of its original members, marched back and stretched out on wet ground in woods just forward of French artillery. The blast of the guns went unnoticed by the men, who slept constantly when they were not enjoying hot meals and coffee. One day they were awakened when two enemy spotting planes, flying so low men on the ground could see the goggles of the pilots and make out the small Iron Crosses painted on the fuselage, were suddenly set afire by a small French Spad. The next day someone bought a Paris *Herald* which proclaimed that the French air ace Captain

René Fonck had destroyed five enemy planes in his greatest day above the Marne.

As soon as the 7th Infantry was in place on June 18 orders came for it to attack, despite the fact that it was in no condition for such an enterprise. Had the Marines known of the order they could have predicted the result, for the Doughboys, like their predecessors, lacked the hand grenades and the heavy artillery support they needed to accomplish the job. In addition, they had not finished their training, and many were raw recruits. Nevertheless, a series of attacks on a battalion scale were begun, and inevitably they failed. Harbord, who had no choice but to follow French orders for persistent attacks, requested one more effort for June 21. "Your battalion will be relieved tomorrow night. Tomorrow morning is its only chance to redeem the failure made this morning. If you clear the northern half of the Bois de Belleau, the credit will belong to the 1st Battalion, 7th Infantry, and will be freely given. The battalion cannot afford to fail again."

At 3:15 A.M. June 21 the attack was launched, the battalion was shattered, and the woods left virtually undefended. Fortunately, the Germans in their own confusion did not realize it before nightfall, and by that time the lice-infested Marines, who had hoped never again to enter Belleau Wood, were moving into its tangled maze once more. Leathernecks began crossing wheat fields in the darkness to reach their positions in the wood. When enemy parachute flares, daylight white, exploded and burned long in the black sky, the long files of Marines had to freeze motionless for fear their moving shadows would betray them. One Doughboy guiding a Marine detachment to its positions was so unnerved by the preceding four nights of horror that he could not restrain the impulse to run when shells burst nearby. This disrupted the column, which could not keep up. The Marine officer finally had to warn him: "Do I have to shoot you to slow you down?" The Doughboy was anguished. "Officer," he cried, "don't shoot me, officer! I got no business here. I only been in the United States Army five weeks." He kept his pace thereafter and found his old position. The next morning in a foxhole his new friends were teaching him how to work the bolt on his Springfield rifle. He begged to stay until he had killed "just one Joiman" but was sent back with a note of thanks to whomever it concerned in the 7th U.S. Infantry.

On June 22, with the Marines back in place, Harbord told Major Shearer, "The situation is intolerable." Harbord's brigade had been driven, inch by inch, into a crescent with its deepest penetration against the last three hundred yards of machine guns in the rocky amphitheater at the northern edge of the wood. The Germans could fire into every trench and foxhole from both flanks. Shearer was ordered to "clear out the woods by tomorrow night." Thus on the afternoon of June 23 the Marines tried again, and, as before, without heavy artillery preparation, the battalion suffered horribly. By eleven o'clock that night the attack was spent, the survivors digging in as the owners of a few more yards of fallen trees, rocky traps, and some captured machine guns. "Things are rather bad. One company almost wiped out," Colonel Neville, the Medal of Honor winner who earlier had said, "Retreat, hell. We just got here," informed General Harbord after midnight. Men in supporting platoons inched forward to plug the gaps in a decimated company, forced to ignore the cries of the wounded for aid because of the desperate urgency of the situation. This was remembered by some survivors as the worst agony of all.

On the morning of the 24th, Lieutentant Colonel Logan Feland slipped through German lines and carried out a perilous reconnaissance as far as the north edge of the wood. When he returned, a briefing was held at Major Shearer's old command post, with General Harbord presiding and the battalion officers in attendance. Feland drew a map showing the curve at the north end of the wood and he told the group that there were no deep trenches there, only rifle pits about six feet deep and twelve feet in length, scattered about three feet apart among boulders that dotted the area. Then plans were made for the next attack to secure the wood, and it was hoped it would be the final one. The attack would take the shape of a fan: the 47th Company in the center, with the longest distance to go; the 20th, plus two platoons of the 45th, on the right; and the 19th on the left. The failure of the previous attack had had one good result; it had convinced French Corps Headquarters that no attack would succeed without proper artillery support. Consequently the attack was put off until 5:15 P.M. the next day, June 25, and the front line of Marines was ordered to pull back two hundred yards so that French and American artillery could shell the woods hard for twenty-four hours. At the end of the briefing Harbord pointed to Feland's map and told the young officer assigned to lead the first wave of the center company, "When you reach the curve, pick up a rifle and lead with steel."

The officer, Laurence Stallings, was twenty-three, and he did not know whether he was a second lieutenant, a first lieutenant, or a captain because of the many losses and field promotions among the line officers. But he was gas-sick, he had a piece of steel in his left leg, and he did not care. Having lost a spiral legging while crawling, he had cut his left breeches leg short, and his beautiful forest-green uniform was held together with strings. He still wore his Sam Browne, deliberately spit-shined to conceal the cowardice he felt at having to wear such an outstanding target, and his cocked Colt .45 was stuffed into his shirt front. His company commander had been badly wounded, and Colonel Neville assigned an old-timer, Capatin Gaines Moseley, to back him up.

That night Stallings and his men moved back, and the shelling began as planned. But the Germans were shelling, too, so fiercely that ration parties carrying hot beef stew could not make their way up "Gob Gully," the supply route. The stew arrived the next morning, cold and sour. Men about to die that afternoon ate it greedily for breakfast.

All day on the 25th big guns continued to plaster the woods in front of the Marine positions, the shelling so severe it did not seem possible any living thing could survive it. At 5:15 the heavy shelling stopped, and there was a moment of silence; then a creeping barrage began to crackle on the mass of brush and fallen trees a hundred yards ahead. Side by side Stallings and his buck sergeant, Alison Page, nephew of President Wilson's ambassador to England, followed by their men, set out to follow the barrage, climbed the bank of a sunken road, and started for the machine guns among the rocks. The moment they stepped out the sergeant was killed by machine gunners beaded on him from four hundred yards away. Stallings and the rest pressed on, Captain Moseley following behind and watching them like a hawk. After the first hundred yards a potato-masher grenade landed at Stallings' feet. He dropped, but not before its explosion had driven fragments of his helmet into his cheek. He got up immediately and pushed on to the rifle pits Colonel Feland had described. He jumped into the first, then fought his way from pit to pit, diving head first from one to the next. The barrage had inflicted very few casualties on the expert German riflemen and Maxim light machine gunners defending their posts, and they fought back stubbornly with no thought of surrender.

About seventy Marines out of two hundred in the 47th Company survived the charge, reached the curve at the north end of the wood, and prepared to dig in to hold the captured position against a German counterattack. At this moment Captain Moseley advised Stallings that Lieutenant Harrison J. Heckman, leading the left platoon of the company, was held up at some boulders short of his objective and had only twenty men left. "You must try to uncover Heckman," said Moseley. "Take as few as you can, begin your demonstration, and I'll get word to Heckman, when he hears you, to go in with what he has left." Stallings took nine men, leaving the rest to hold the curve, and moved west by south, now out of the woods. He could hear the yells and shots of Heckman and his twenty men as they followed Moseley's order to charge (Heckman and two of his men would survive), but Stallings had not gone two hundred yards when he came under the fire of about 150 German troops of the counterassault teams and was struck in the leg. Half an hour later, his shattered leg well tourniqueted, he sat up and gave Major Ralph Keyser of the leapfrog battalion the Germans' exact position, and soon he heard the shouts, shots, and screams of the mopping up.

In the aftermath there was only a broken wood of second-growth timber where dead men lay around rocky nests, both Germans and Americans slumped across machine guns, trails of wounded leading farther on to the edge of the forest. The U.S. Navy's hospital corpsmen swarmed all through the wood, here and there a captured German medic aiding, crying "*Langsam . . . langsam* (slowly . . . slowly)" to prisoners lifting Yanks on stretchers made by slinging a blanket between two Mauser rifles, barrels still hot from the intense fire directed at the Leathernecks. From time to time shots, screams, and battlefield yells told where mopping up continued in the twilight of isolated glades and wooded patches. Around nine o'clock Colonel Neville sent a message to Harbord: "Woods now *U.S. Marine Corps* entirely."

Harbord was sick of slaughter. In a moment of indulgence he had permitted his headquarters first sergeant and his favorite messman, always begging for a chance to see some action, to participate in the attack, and now he had to send out searchers to find their bodies. He had never ceased to be concerned about officers getting themselves killed in droves—they were so hard to replace—and now the 3rd Battalion was almost bereft of them. Even the last of the young Doughboy officers, lent the battalion to take the place of fallen Marines, had been killed. Harbord read Neville's message. Words like "glory" were not in his vocabulary. He merely replied: "Your Shearer Battalion has done splendid work." And this was the capture of Belleau Wood.

There were many views as to the value of the stand at Belleau Wood and its eventual capture. (It was also pointed out that it could have been taken in fifteen minutes with the help of British Mark IV tanks, but they were never available to the Yanks.) It was certainly a morale booster for the failing French, who had suffered 400,000 casualties since March 21. But it has been claimed—by General Robert L. Bullard, for one, who of all the Americans knew the French best—that had not the 2nd Division blocked access to the Paris road on May 31 the war would have been over, for the Germans would have been able to cross the Marne at will west of Château-Thierry and encircle the defensive line to the east. German orders and actions bear this out. Only on June 8, after five days of constant and unsuccessful attacks in which they were brutally molested by the Americans, did the Germans call off their offensive and assume the defensive.

"In the fighting on our front," German General Conta had warned, "should the Americans even temporarily gain the upper hand, it would have the most unfavorable aspect for us as regards the morale of the Allies and the duration of the war." Conta ordered that "this or that unimportant wood or village" (Belleau Wood or Bouresches) was to be retaken whenever Americans captured it. And Lieutenant von Buy, a German intellectual of the General Staff, was impressed by the showing of the Americans and by the prisoners from the 2nd Division whom he examined. "The various attacks by both of the Marine regiments were carried out with vigor and regardless of losses. The effect of our firearms did not materially check the advance of the infantry. The nerves of the Americans are still unshaken. . . . The personnel may be considered excellent. The spirit of the troops is fresh and one of careless confidence. A characteristic expression of one of the prisoners is 'We kill or get killed.' . . . Only a few of them are genuine Americans by ancestry, the majority is of German, Dutch, or Italian parentage; but these half-Americans, who with few exceptions were born in America, and who never before had been in Europe, consider themselves unhesitatingly as genuine sons of America." This may have been amazing to Lieutenant von Buy, but it was the assumption of John J. Pershing and every Doughboy in his command.

Private Bailey had seen the last of the war ten days earlier on June 15. He and his buddies in the 9th Infantry's 3rd Battalion lay in reserve on the right flank in a state of inaction while their friends were fighting and dying. They felt waiting was more trying than the trial of combat itself. The Germans had brought heavy guns into play, ranging and searching the wooded patches for Bailey and his friends. Bailey heard one of their heavy shells coming that evening, and described what happened.

> There was something unusual about the sound of this particular shell. It seemed to be coming closer than the general run of shells. I was certain that no shell could fall in this sheltered spot but I thought it best not to trust my judgment too far. Then I considered whether I would try to get to my dugout or lie down where I was and take my chances. . . . I decided I would try for my dugout. . . . I was diving through the air and just as I was about to disappear . . . the shell exploded. . . . I felt a stinging sensation in my right elbow. . . . At noon the nurse came around and told me I was to have the dressing on my wound changed. . . . I looked and saw that the little hole that had been there the night before had been enlarged to a cut that extended from a couple of inches below the elbow nearly to my shoulder and was into the bone.

Three days later, strolling in pink pajamas and robe outside the hospital gates, he saw some rookies from the 4th Division trying to make head or tail out of French Chauchats they had just been issued together with instructions in French. Private Bailey's fighting days were over, but he continued to serve; he sat on the ground and with one arm showed his new friends how to affix a half-moon clip of flimsy construction to that beastly-looking weapon.

During the fighting at Belleau Wood there was fierce loyalty between the Doughboy and Marine brigades of the 2nd Division. But there was fierce rivalry, too, each brigade trying to outdo the other until, like a pair of high-spirited horses, they were known as the racehorse brigades. There was an incident on June 6: a Leatherneck runner, encountering a Doughboy military policeman, asked the M.P. why he was so near the front. "To keep you Marines from running away," said the Doughboy. They were still rolling in the dirt when an ambulance crew pried them apart.

This rivalry was not eased when, through a censor's slip, the

Marines were identified in the Paris *Herald* as fighting in Belleau Wood. This was the first and last mention of an infantry group by designation, but it was splashed over the front page of papers in every city in America, the implication being that no one but Marines was fighting in the Château-Thierry area. The Doughboys were understandably angry. Pershing knew the fanfare would cause every Doughboy sergeant in France—Regular, National Guard, or draftee—to die rather than suffer by comparison to the Marines.

The Doughboy Brigade got its chance to shine on the night of July 1 in an attack on the town of Vaux, one mile to the west of Château-Thierry. The 23rd Infantry was assigned the Bois de la Roche on the left. Only lightly shelled, the woods would prove costly to the Yanks. Soldiers of the 9th Infantry, their target Vaux, knew the nature and location of every machine-gun pit ringing the town, every house in it, and some even knew the names of the occupants, long since fled.

The Vaux attack went off with dash and style. Colonel Malone of the 23rd Infantry directed it, and the Doughboys displayed much daring on the wooded flanks where the French, made cautious by four years of terrible losses, failed to move up in time. When a French machine-gun outfit, arriving tardily, tried to claim some Germans captured by the Doughboys, a Yank Lieutenant overrode his sergeant's objections. "Oh, let 'em keep 'em. We'll catch some more." Many were the battalion's gallant exploits that night in the crumbling streets of Vaux and in the woods to its left. No one ever knew how many Doughboys from the rear areas joined the assault teams; engineers, signalers, artillerymen, and mule skinners played hookey and went along in a show of their own, stung by the maddening headline about the Marines in the Paris *Herald*. "We have fought the Canadians and the Australians," a captured German officer said, "but you fellows are rougher." Everyone beamed, and the German was showered with cigarettes.

Violence on the Marne

During the weeks of June in which the U.S. 2nd and 3rd Divisions were holding the line at Belleau Wood and Château-Thierry, French divisions rushed up by General Foch had managed to stem the German armies on the western and eastern flanks of the May 27 German breakthrough. When the Germans were finally stopped, their penetration into French lines formed a salient that, on a map, roughly resembled a deep bowl. The base or deepest line of advance ran along the Marne River from Château-Thierry to a point about fifteen miles east. The eastern side curved up from the Marne to Reims, and the western side angled more sharply through Vaux and Belleau Wood toward Soissons (see map, page 43). The depth and width of the salient were both about thirty miles at the maximum.

General Foch, now a Marshal of France as well as supreme commander of all Allied forces, realized that the German bulge protruding below the stabilized front line on either flank was vulnerable to an Allied counterattack. He began to plan secretly in June for an assault in July, placing particular emphasis on recapturing Soissons. Through this city ran the railroad to Reims and one of the two highways supplying the German armies thirty miles to the south.

Foch also guessed that his brilliant opponent, General Erich Ludendorff, would plan another strike to exploit his latest success, but he did not expect the Germans would be ready to attack again before July 20. Hoping to beat the Germans to the punch, Foch picked July 18 for his attack. He would need all the time available until then to recover from the series of defeats he had suffered since March, reorganize his shattered divisions, call up reserves, and switch over to the offensive. From March through June, 1918, the French had lost 400,000 men killed, wounded, and missing. (During the same period less than 100,000 Americans had taken part in active fighting.) The Germans had suffered, too, but they still held a distinct advantage in manpower. Their armies in France, reinforced by divisions from the now quiet Eastern Front, were at a peak strength of three and a half million men, outnumbering the British and French by some 600,000 troops.

Foch came to Chaumont in June to see what Pershing could do about this manpower shortage. Pershing did not have much to offer beyond those American divisions already engaged—the 1st, 2nd, 3rd, and 26th. The rest of his Doughboy divisions in France were still very new and very green, but he agreed to help in every way possible and he gave Foch a list of American divisions whose training was most nearly completed.

A few weeks after their conference Foch sent Pershing his plans for using the Americans in the weeks ahead. The 1st and 2nd Divisions, now battle tested, would be sent to rest areas below the Marne where their depleted ranks would be filled with replacements and they could begin training for Foch's counter-offensive of July 18. The 26th Division of New Englanders, who had tasted their first combat at Seicheprey, would be transferred from that part of the front to replace the 2nd Division in the Belleau Wood area. The 42nd Rainbow Division, a National Guard outfit whose soldiers came from twenty-six states, would be assigned to back up French divisions on the eastern flank of the German bulge near Reims. The untried 28th Division of the Pennsylvania National Guard was given a supporting role, too, backing up a French division on the Marne line eight miles east of Château-Thierry. Just to the left of this French division and the Pennsylvanians was the U.S. 3rd Division which had been holding down some seven miles of Marne River front from Château-Thierry to the village of Varennes since early June. Foch ordered the 3rd Division to stay there and build up its defenses in the event the Germans attacked.

The commander of the 3rd Division was the able Major General Joseph T. Dickman, a portly cavalryman with a painter's eye for landscapes, a gourmet's taste for wines, and a soldier's eye for ground. Dickman took stock of the terrain in his sector and quickly concluded that the most likely spot for a possible German assault was on his right, where there was a square mile of wheat field, wooded patches, and small ravines between the river and the open plain of Le Rocq. The mile-deep Rocq Plateau, Dickman knew, would be greatly prized by the Germans as an assembly ground for their troops if they ever crossed the Marne, so he decided to let them cross the river and fight for this pleatau against what he considered his prize infantry regiment, the 38th.

Dickman chose the 38th to defend this sector of the line because of his confidence in its commanding officer, Colonel Ulysses Grant McAlexander, a pugnacious and fearless Texan. (Visitors to the state capitol in Austin will find a portrait of the colonel in a place of honor.) Before joining the 3rd Division as commander of the 38th Infantry, McAlexander had been assigned to the 1st Division, and General Bullard had sacked him for his profane refusal to believe the French could tell him anything about war. Before McAlexander left the Marne the Germans would find him equally stubborn; on just one fantastic day there, he and his 38th Infantry Regiment would earn the nickname "The Rock of the Marne."

In preparing for a possible German attack, McAlexander refused to listen to French advice that he place most of his men close to the river and try to prevent the Germans from crossing over. He knew German artillery could make a shambles of his defenses if he bunched his men too far forward, and he preferred to build a trap and let the German infantry into it. There was a railroad line on a raised embankment that ran parallel to the river a few hundred yards south of it. McAlexander hid two of his three battalions south of the railroad line as reserves for counterassault teams, and he committed only one battalion to the river side of the railroad embankment.

McAlexander's next consideration was his flanks. To his immediate right was the French division supported by the U.S. 28th Division, with many other French divisions further east along the Marne line. The colonel knew that in the event of a German attack the French would fall back, yielding ground to save lives. He felt no bitterness about it, telling his young captains that in time, if the war lasted, Americans would also yield ground, but that in this first test it was important they hold firm.

To protect his right flank McAlexander had his men dig slit trenches facing east. He assigned F Company of the 2nd Battalion, commanded by a shy fellow with the build of a fullback, Captain T. C. Reid, to hold the position.

The 38th's left flank adjoined the 30th Infantry of the 3rd Division. McAlexander was convinced that this flank, too, would be a priority target for the Germans, and he selected the company of Captain Jesse W. Wooldridge, a young San Franciscan with glasses and a sandy-haired pompadour, to hold it. Between Wooldridge on the left and Reid on the right, McAlexander placed companies H and E of the 2nd Battalion.

Except for Reid's company, McAlexander gave his company commanders carte blanche to position their platoons. Wooldridge did not believe any German colonel foolish enough to attempt a charge through the waist-high, poppy-flecked wheat in the fields facing him. He placed only one platoon, under Lieutenant Calkins, in the thick brush at the river's edge, pledged to fight there until overrun. His second platoon was assigned to the river side of the railroad embankment behind Calkins, deep in holes near its leading edge, and his third was dug in behind the railroad. His fourth

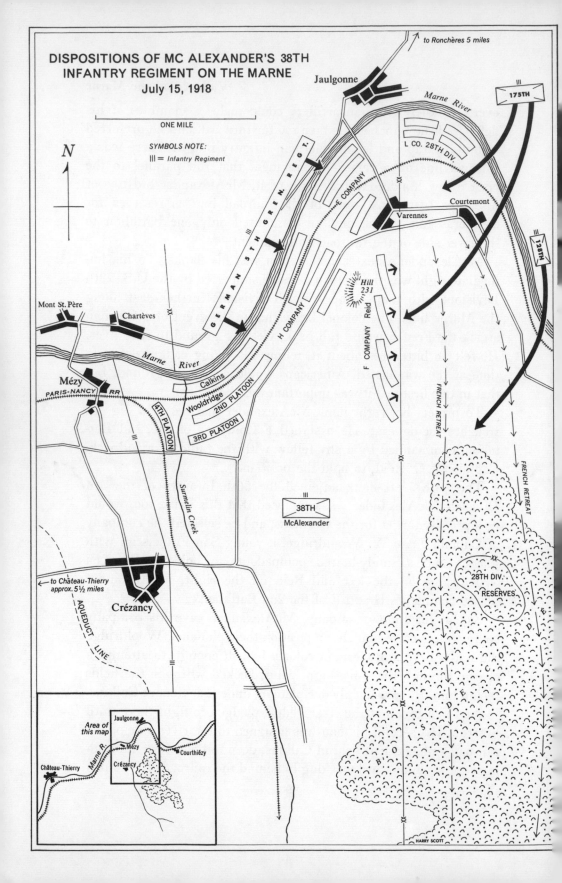

DISPOSITIONS OF MC ALEXANDER'S 38TH INFANTRY REGIMENT ON THE MARNE
July 15, 1918

ONE MILE

N

SYMBOLS NOTE:
III = Infantry Regiment

to Ronchères 5 miles

Jaulgonne

Marne River

175TH

L CO. 28TH DIV.

GERMAN 5TH GREN. REGT.

E COMPANY

Courtemont

Varennes

128TH

Hill 231

Reid

H COMPANY

F COMPANY

FRENCH RETREAT

FRENCH RETREAT

Mont St. Père

Chartèves

Marne River

Calkins

Wooldridge

4TH PLATOON

2ND PLATOON

3RD PLATOON

Mézy

PARIS-NANCY RR

Surmelin Creek

38TH
McAlexander

28TH DIV. RESERVES

to Château-Thierry approx. 5½ miles

Crézancy

AQUEDUCT LINE

B O I S   D E   C O N D E

Area of this map

Jaulgonne

Marne R.

Mézy

Crézancy

Château-Thierry

Courthiézy

HARRY SCOTT

platoon was entrenched on a railroad spur jutting southeast from the main line and protecting his flank. The captains of H and E companies each ordered two platoons to the river's edge and two astride the railroad.

Wooldridge had no idea how his men would hold up under fire. None had ever been in battle before. Private Wilson was a wealthy boy from New York whose father frequently had visited training camp to demand his son's discharge. Acting Corporal Enright was a troublemaker continually griping because sergeants pushed ahead of him in chow line. There was a Private Dickman from New York, a recent immigrant who spoke little English and seemed to possess two left feet. There was also the company water cart driver, a peewee with an unpronounceable name, whom Wooldridge regarded as absolutely useless. The captain hoped that when the fighting started Peewee would be two miles back of the line with his cart, where his mule would no doubt block the road, ignoring the blasphemies of a French staff officer whose limousine was held up.

But there were others, like Corporal Connors, assigned to guard the river bank under Lieutenant Calkins, whom Wooldridge had taught all he had learned from Colonel McAlexander, who was every inch the soldier. In the weeks the 38th Infantry had been in position the colonel had been over every foot of ground, often walking erect in daytime in plain sight of German gunners across the river. Sergeants who did not recognize him would shout, "Get down, you crazy idiot!" or "Get down, you goddam fool!" When they recognized their colonel and stood agape, he would say breezily, "When you get to be a colonel, son, you can go where you please." He was a fabulously popular West Pointer, and he had his "melting pot" regiment as well prepared as he could get it for a possible German onslaught.

During the weeks of late June and early July it was relatively quiet along the front from Soissons to Reims. The German juggernaut had been stopped for a time, and both sides strengthened their lines and waited for the next move. Overhead, Allied and German planes dueled for control of the sky, and there were a number of Americans, flying French pursuit craft and photo-reconnaissance planes, whose job was to try to find hidden German troops. By this time romance and gallantry had all but gone out of the air war; it was a grim business of kill or be killed, as it was on the ground.

In the second week of July, Harvard graduate Douglas Campbell, a fighter pilot, became the first American ace when he made his fifth kill above Château-Thierry. His victim was a Rumpler two-seater observation craft. When Campbell approached it, the German observer in the rear seat stood up with arms folded in the traditional signal that he was out of ammunition. Earlier in the war Campbell would have gallantly spared his opponents' lives, but now he could not risk letting them get their photographs of American positions to German artillerymen. He tried to get the German fliers to follow him as captives to a French field, but when they failed to acknowledge his signals he shot them down.

A few days later Quentin Roosevelt, the youngest son of ex-President Theodore Roosevelt, was shot down and killed behind German lines not far from Château-Thierry. Quentin, who had just finished his pilot training, had been flying the position known as "tail-end Charlie"—the last aviator in a flight—in an American squadron of French Spads. Just as his squadron mates sighted a flight of red-nosed German Fokkers and swept forward to meet them head on, Quentin spotted another flight of about a dozen Fokkers over his right shoulder. Undaunted by the odds against him, Quentin broke formation and began his turn and climb to meet the enemy—and certain death—with his single plane. The Germans buried him with military honors near the village of Chamery, honors paid not only because they remembered and admired the Rough Rider President, but also because they knew it needed guts to meet death that way.

On the ground during this time of waiting there was a great deal of patrol action, something every Doughboy wanted to take part in, and both Yanks and Germans sent small groups across the lines as scouting parties. It was because of a daring patrol on July 14 on the front near Reims, where the 42nd Division was in support, that one of the greatest pieces of good fortune ever to bless any army fell into Foch's hands.

A German major was captured whose papers revealed the time and plan of the German attack. Instead of July 20 or later, as Foch had anticipated, Ludendorff had selected that very midnight, July 14-15, as his H-hour. Once again the able Ludendorff had beaten Foch to the punch with an offensive. It was to be a massive assault on a front of some eighty miles, from Château-Thierry in the west to Verdun in the east, with the major effort across the Marne. If the Germans could breach the defenses near Château-Thierry they would be only a short distance from Paris (see map, page 43). German artillery was to open its bombardment at ten minutes past midnight. On the Marne front fourteen German divisions under von Boehn would begin crossing the river at 1:30 A.M., attacking the U.S. 3rd Division and the French divisions east of it, with fourteen more to follow at daylight. East of Reims two other German armies would hurl themselves forward against the French defenses. It was all excellently planned, and the Germans were very optimistic.

Foch put his faith in this piece of information and gambled that the captured major and his papers were not a German trick. A quarter of an hour before midnight every Allied battery south of the Marne opened on the German troops who were hurrying in the night to the north bank of the river. Had Foch guessed wrong he would thus have revealed the whereabouts of his own massed guns and subjected them to destruction by German artillery in the days ahead. The French had twenty-five agonizing minutes to wait. Then brilliant star shells burst above French and American lines, and, on schedule, German artillery crashed in reply.

Despite the punishment many German regiments received in the unexpected French and American bombardment, on the Marne front von Boehn's men began launching their pontoon boats from the north bank of the river as early as 1:10 A.M.

To the right of the 3rd Division the French fought frantically for a short while and then, as McAlexander had predicted, started for the rear. Captain T. C. Reid, the shy captain with the build of a fullback, whose company was guarding the 38th's right flank, saw soldiers streaming south in the half-darkness of early dawn. Reid thought they were retreating French and let them pass. He discovered with daylight that the French had long since left without notifying him and he had been watching German grenadiers slip past. So deep was the German penetration of the neighboring French division's lines that there was little hope of support for Reid from the 38th's second line battalion, now heavily engaged on its own flank and rear.

But on the 38th's left flank, where Captain Jesse W. Wooldridge's company was dug in, there was no falling back. As German infantry in their pontoon boats approached the south bank of the river they came under fire from Doughboys like Lieutenant Calkins and Corporal Connors in the brush along the river's edge. The Germans returned the fire from their boats, hitting many Yanks, and kept coming. Calkins was shot down and wounded at 2 A.M., and his platoon was overrun by enemy infantry wading ashore. The wounded lieutenant was ferried across the river by his German captors and given first aid, and he survived.

Corporal Connors with his squad of two Chauchat teams and their buddies from three companies killed twenty boatloads of Germans before all the Americans but Connors were killed or wounded. Connors had no more ammunition for his hiccuping Chauchats, but there were still the grenades. He began throwing these into the oncoming boats rather than retire with honor to his company line on the railway embankment, and he was finally killed by a German rifleman. All five platoons on the bank were overwhelmed or annihilated, but they had bought precious time and had compelled two regiments of German Grenadier Guards to change their course.

Nevertheless, the Germans kept pouring across the river, and just before dawn two thirds of a German division were on the south bank of the Marne. Their next step was to wait for daylight and then storm the railway embankment. When daylight came they began working their way forward through the wheat in combat groups with their automatic riflemen and machine gunners covering them. As soon as they were within throwing range, the advancing line of storm troops hurled their grenades and charged.

The first shock of the German assault, led by a captain of the 5th Grenadiers, was met by Lieutenant Mercer M. Phillips of Wooldridge's right platoon. Phillips, the biggest man in the 38th, was wounded in the head, and as Corporal Desoldart knelt to bandage his forehead, the German captain was upon them. Phillips was up in a flash with the corporal's rifle, bayoneting the German who, as he fell, put a pistol bullet in the giant Doughboy lieutenant's brain.

The Germans failed to carry the embankment on this try, but they had succeeded in working closer to it, and they began setting up some of their machine guns at almost point-blank range. A short time after this first charge Wooldridge found he had to counterattack a German machine gun on his right flank with a half-platoon commanded by Lieutenant Paul Murray. The thin line of perhaps twenty men began wriggling through the wheat, pausing to fire, waiting for the signal to rise and go in with the bayonet. Doughboys were dropping all along the line, and when two men between Wooldridge and Murray were killed, Wooldridge crawled over to the lieutenant and shouted that they must keep the right flank up or all was lost. His arm was around Murray when a bullet crushed the lieutenant's brains. Wooldridge, searching for survivors, found only one man left alive, Private Weiner. Together they charged the machine gun, and with the last bullet of his last clip Woolridge killed the German machine-gun officer who had caused all the trouble. Weiner forced the surrender of the three surviving German gunners with his bayonet, and captain and private returned to their lines with their prisoners.

Because of such American exploits, things were not going well for the German Grenadiers. Their two regiments had been unable to join up, and both their general and the colonel of the 6th Grenadiers had been shot. It was suicide for a German to raise his head "above the ears" in the wheat, one of them said afterward. Wooldridge soon killed the staff major of the leading German battalion as well. He was not of a mind to kill him at first; he merely shot him in the right hand before the German could pull his pistol from its holster. The major, staring at Wooldridge, then slowly moved his left hand across his body to the butt of his pistol. Wooldridge started to raise his knee to boot the fellow to the ground, but the heat of battle was on him and, when the German still tried to draw his pistol, he killed him instead.

A Doughboy nearby bayoneted the German major's adjutant, who uttered a loud "Ugh!" Shortly afterward, Wooldridge was astonished to see that one of his least reliable men, the peewee of the water cart who had indeed been behind the lines, had made his way on foot two miles through the bombardment, and was now wearing the Luger pistol of a German staff officer. An American staff officer later admired it, and the runt of the 38th's litter presented it to him. "Did you kill him?" asked the officer. "Did I kill him? Why, you could hang your pack on my bayonet sticking through his back!" That was the "Ugh!" Wooldridge had heard.

It was that kind of a fight all through the morning and into the afternoon: brutal, bitter, hand-to-hand struggles between individuals and small groups, and there was valor on both sides. In the heat of the fray a corporal brought a Prussian officer to Wooldridge. As the captain came forward to search him for information the Prussian drew his battle orders from his jacket as if to tear them up. Woodridge jammed a pistol in his belly. The German, looking the American in the eyes, tore the papers into bits. Wooldridge let the brave man keep his life and sent him to the rear. Another time, in the midst of one battle, Wooldridge found McAlexander between him and the enemy. The captain scolded him: "Colonel, don't you know that nothing can live in this place?" McAlexander shrugged his oxlike shoulders. "Well, while anyone is left alive, let's give them hell."

Wooldridge had the opportunity to observe many of the doubtful rookies in action, and he later wrote about his company. Private

Wilson, the New York society boy, was observed by Wooldridge in a slit trench with two buddies when three German Grenadiers got to him. He saw Wilson bayonet the first man, have his rifle wrested away from him by a second, saw him retrieve it from the German and kill him. The third he knocked down with his fist and claimed as prisoner.

Enright, the troublemaker who hated senior noncoms, led a flank movement against five German machine-gun positions. When the operation was completed, he brought back his two wounded buddies and thirty-six prisoners, pretty well shot up. However, he had forgotten to destroy the German machine guns so that they would be useless if they fell into German hands again, and he knew the old noncoms would needle him for this. Unable to bear this thought, Acting Corporal Enright seized an entrenching tool, went back alone, and disabled the guns by smashing their sights.

Wooldridge got around to Private Dickman, the recently arrived immigrant who was in his reserve platoon. The private was in a slit trench with two men who had learned musketry by firing at tomato cans and knew nothing about allowing for distance, elevation, and wind direction. To Wooldridge's amazement he heard Dickman calling ranges, and he watched him firing carefully and coaching the others like a Regular Army man. No German ever lived long enough to reach that slit trench.

The most surprising of the lot was a man named Richardson and nicknamed "Eaglebeak" after a comic-strip character of the time patterned on Washington Irving's Ichabod Crane. Eaglebeak never seemed strong enough to lift a camp stool, and no amount of gymnastics had ever been able to put an ounce on his skinny frame. But today, in his first countercharge, Eaglebeak swept upon a German machine gunner with his bayonet. The German promptly took the rifle away from him. To Wooldridge, Eaglebeak looked like a goner, but he closed with the enemy, rolling in the wheat, and beat the gunner to his pistol. There was a muffled report, and the emaciated Eaglebeak arose, possessor of a Luger pistol, the proudest trophy a Doughboy could display.

So it went throughout the day. As early as 6 A.M., McAlexander had committed his second-line battalion and was ordering up his third. As the morning wore on, literally everyone was involved in small battles on both sides of the railroad, in clumps of woods, in wheat fields, small ravines, or on the Rocq Plateau. A belligerent mess sergeant named O'Connor and an equally fierce chief cook named Maloney abandoned their rolling stoves in exposed places in the rear and joined Wooldridge in the front line, fighting with fury. German gunners shot the kitchens to pieces, thinking they were field guns. As a result, it was four days after the battle before the company had a hot meal. The company's survivors subsisted on horsemeat goulash until Mess Sergeant O'Connor and Chief Cook Maloney "acquired" some French rolling kitchens and large stocks of corned-beef hash and canned tomatoes for a mulligan stew.

"Why're ya makin' so much hash, Sergeant?" asked one of Wooldridge's men.

"Listen, buddy, hash ain't no orchid that has to be worn the same day!"

Captain Reid on the 38th's right flank had much the same experience throughout the day as Wooldridge on the left. The fighting there was so furious that several times the battalion's surgeon, Captain Daniels, dropped his instruments and, with field medics and wounded, joined Reid's men to drive off enemy combat teams. On one such occasion the ever-present McAlexander appeared and was chided for exposing himself. "Well," he replied, "I suppose I should be about twenty miles back with a bunch of orderlies around me and a telephone to tell you fellows what to do. But, hell, I want to see what's going on."

Reid's company was cut off from the regiment much of the time by German penetration, and suffered heavy losses. McAlexander managed to send Reid replacements in driblets, and more than once the captain picked out men he had never seen before and made them corporals on the field to lead squads in counterattacks. For his last counterattack, around five o'clock in the afternoon, he threw in his cooks, clerks, bottlewashers, and typists. The company cook led the last charge, for the mess sergeant had been shot, vainly trying to rescue a pal. "My men were magnificent," Reid wrote later, "easily handled, trustworthy, ready and willing to take any chance I would take with them. Their rifle fire was accurate, bayonet fighting furious, and valor simply indescribable." Reid was a square peg in a square hole that day, another example of McAlexander's uncanny ability to pick the right man for the right job. Reid's only regret, expressed later, was that he had not, like Wooldridge, killed any Germans himself. "Colonel," he wrote to McAlexander, "I was just too busy."

By nightfall on July 15 the fighting in the 3rd Division's sector was virtually over. The German grenadier regiments that had crossed the Marne that morning were shattered, the survivors huddled by the river waiting to be ferried back to the north bank under cover of darkness. It was a staggering setback to German hopes. Had they been able to take the Rocq Plateau from McAlexander and his men they might have swept on toward Paris and ended the war. The performance of the 3rd Division, and particularly of the men of McAlexander's 38th Infantry, had been magnificent.

The Germans fared slightly better against the French divisions to the right of these Doughboys. The French retreat that Captain T. C. Reid had witnessed in the pre-dawn hours of July 15 permitted the Germans to penetrate French defenses to a depth of about three miles, and it took the French three days to drive the attackers back across the Marne.

To the northeast, along the eastern face of the German salient and from Reims eastward, where two other German armies had charged forward in the early hours of July 15, the results were similar. On the first day the attackers gained three or four miles, but their losses were heavy and they were unable to score a breakthrough. That night and all through the daylight hours of July 16 the exhausted and exposed survivors among the German shock troops were pounded by French artillery and subjected to repeated counter-charges by French reserves. After two days of this beating the German generals called off the attack and ordered their men to return to their original lines.

The defeat of the German offensive of July 15 was the first German setback in 1918 after three resounding victories. The battle was both a high-water mark for the Germans, and a turning point in the fortunes of the war. Never again would German soldiers set foot on the south side of the Marne or get so close to Paris. With the Germans thwarted at last, the initiative for the next move finally had passed to Major General Ferdinand Foch and the Allies.

Chapter

8

Soissons: The Road Back

GENERAL FOCH'S RESOLVE to launch a counteroffensive on July 18 never faltered in the face of the surprise German assault of July 15. When one of his subordinates expressed doubts Foch replied sharply, "There can be no question at all of slowing up, and less so of stopping, the . . . operation." His plans had been made carefully and secretly for weeks, with highest priority assigned to cutting the supply road from Soissons to the Marne. If this artery could be cut, German resistance to the south might collapse (see map, page 80).

For the attack near Soissons, Foch chose the best assault troops he had available, the U.S. 1st and 2nd Divisions and the French 1st (Moroccan) Division, supported by what was left of the French Foreign Legion. The French commander knew from the performance of the Yanks at Cantigny and Belleau Wood that the survivors of these outfits were first-class fighting men. Now rested, their ranks brought up to full strength by replacements, each of these American divisions was numerically about twice the size of a French division. In addition, the American soldier was physically bigger and stronger than the French poilu and

77

had more endurance for an advance with rifle, bayonet, and heavy pack.

Foch assigned the 1st Division to positions just west of Soissons, and the 2nd Division a few miles south of the 1st. He placed the Moroccans between them. The Moroccans wore red fezzes and, as they were Moslems, were accompanied by mullahs (holy men) who preached that Allah was merciful. They were the best French assault troops that Foch had left.

The Yanks of the 1st and 2nd Divisions knew they were going to fight when their artillery began pulling out from below the Marne as early as July 13. They did not know their destination, but it mattered little to them. The past few weeks they had been catching up on lost sleep, enjoying hot food, and getting to know the new men. The replacements included National Guardsmen from the Pacific coast and thousands of draftees, including a battalion of government clerks from the District of Columbia.

There were some interesting promotions among the higher officers. General Bullard moved up from command of the 1st Division to command of a corps of several divisions, with General Summerall, who had been in charge of artillery at Cantigny, taking his place as leader of the Big Red One. Harbord, who had led the Marine Brigade at Belleau Wood, took over command of the 2nd Division, giving the post he was leaving to his new friend, Neville, the Medal of Honor winner from the 5th Marine Regiment. Perhaps the most interesting new face belonged to the new commander of the Doughboy infantry brigade of the 2nd Division, Brigadier General Hanson E. Ely. This tough fighter had been rewarded for the fine job he had done in the Cantigny assault.

As the night of July 17-18 fell, Doughboys of the 1st and 2nd Divisions assembled southwest of Soissons under cover of darkness in the forests of Retz and Villers-Cotterêts. Many regiments had been without food or water for twenty-four hours, and they were burdened with heavy packs and carrying extra bandoliers of ammunition. As they moved forward along uncharted trails, through dense forest under sheets of rain, many platoons got

President Woodrow Wilson
Premier Georges Clemenceau

Major General John J. Pershing
Marshal Ferdinand Foch

Field Marshal Sir Douglas Haig

Kaiser Wilhelm II

Field Marshal Paul von Hindenburg

General Erich Ludendorff

Four who won their country's highest award, the Medal of Honor. Above, left, Lt. Col. William (Wild Bill) Donovan of The Fighting Sixty-Ninth, 42nd Division; right, Sgt. Alvin C. York. Below, left, 2nd Lt. Frank Luke, the "Arizona Balloon Buster," who was awarded the Medal posthumously; right, Lt. Col. Charles W. Whittlesey of the Lost Battalion receiving the award from Maj. Gen. Clarence Edwards.

Some of those who won Pershing's accolade—"He is a fighter . . . a fighter . . . a fighter!"—pose with him and his staff at Chaumont after the Armistice. Singled out by number are: (1) Capt. George C. McMurtry of the Lost Battalion, (2) Maj. Gen. Charles P. Summerall, (3) Maj. Gen. James W. McAndrew, Chief of Staff, (4) Maj. Gen. Hunter Liggett, (5) Capt. George H. Mallon, who used a right to the jaw to capture a machine-gun position near the Meuse, (6) Gen. Pershing, (7) Maj. Gen. Robert L. Bullard, (8) Cpl. [now 2nd Lt.] Donald M. Call, tank driver at Varennes, (9) Lt. Samuel Woodfill, outstanding "Old Army" soldier of the war, (10) Brig. Gen. Dennis E. Nolan, Intelligence Chief, (11) Cpl. Frank T. Bart, whose short legs grew tired carrying messages at Blanc Mont.

Cantigny, May 28, 1918. The first American attack of the war. Above, Dough-boys of the 28th Infantry, 1st Division, go "over the top." Below, the bridge at Château-Thierry. The bridge over the Marne was blown up by French engineers on June 1, 1918, while French and German troops were still fighting for it. The German breakthrough at the Chemin des Dames was stopped here, and the U.S. 3rd Division dug in on the south bank and held the Marne line for six weeks.

Above, Belleau Wood. In this tangled forest three miles west of Château-Thierry, the Marine Brigade of the 2nd Division fought the Germans to a standstill for three weeks, finally capturing the Wood on June 25, 1918. Below, the ruins of Vaux. The town, between Belleau Wood and Château-Thierry, was photographed a few weeks after its capture on July 1, 1918, by the Doughboy Brigade of the 2nd Division.

These pictures show the aftermath of von Boehn's attack against McAlexander's 38th Infantry Regiment positions. Above, left, German dead and equipment in U.S. lines; right, two dead Doughboy machine gunners; below, captured German arms.

Foch's counterattack against the German bulge on the Marne. Above, German infantry flee their positions near Soissons, where the U.S. 1st and 2nd divisions went into action against them. Below, field artillery near Vaux moves forward. For the next six weeks, American and French troops fought their way through the Champagne country from the Marne to the Aisne River.

On September 12, the first all-American Army offensive was launched at Saint-Mihiel. Above, men of the 3rd Division advance toward Montsec. Below, U.S. artillerymen work their French 75 as fast as it can be loaded and fired. Empty shell casings litter the ground behind them.

The Saint-Mihiel campaign was relatively easy, but only two weeks later the Doughboys had to be in position to assault powerful German defenses in the Meuse-Argonne sector sixty miles to the northwest. Above, a German trench; below, U.S. engineers struggle to repair a shelled road in terrain "as desolate as the moon."

On September 26, the Meuse-Argonne offensive began, the American First Army attacking along a twenty-five mile front. Above, Doughboys of the 77th Division rest in a captured German trench in the Argonne Forest; below, in the marshes near the Meuse, infantrymen of the 33rd Division take temporary shelter in a shallow trench.

One of the biggest jobs of the war was to keep the fighting men supplied. Above, a supply train moves up to the front. This was the kind of organized confusion that upset Premier Clemenceau. Below, a German Fokker shot down behind American lines while attacking an observation balloon.

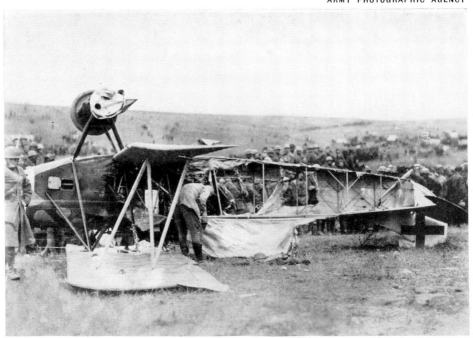

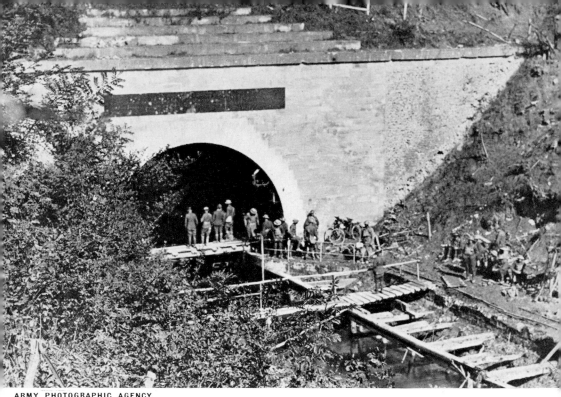

In the British sector far to the west of the Meuse-Argonne, Doughboys of the 27th and 30th divisions stormed the Saint-Quentin Tunnel complex in the Hindenburg Line on September 29. Above, the entrance to the tunnel shortly after it was captured; below, a view of the canal showing German dugouts in its steep bank.

While the British and French were making better progress in their sectors against crumbling German opposition, the desperate Germans fought stubbornly to stop Americans in the Meuse-Argonne from breaking through to Sedan. Above, Doughboys crawl up Hill 240 near Exermont; below, some of the survivors of the Lost Battalion.

On October 14, the American First Army launched a massive attack on the Kriemhilde Stellung of the German's Hindenburg Line. It was October 27 before the town of Grandpré, shown above, was captured, after fierce fighting on its terraced slopes. Below, the view from a captured German machine-gun position above Grandpré.

The final assault of the American First Army, on November 1, met determined resistance at first. Then the Yanks broke through the Freya Stellung and pushed on toward Sedan against dwindling opposition. Above, Americans marching through the captured town of Stenay; below, a high German observation point, occupied by a smiling Doughboy after the Armistice.

mixed up in spite of the efforts of platoon leaders to hold their sixty shivering men together. The old-timers knew they were going to attack at 4:45 in the morning, following a rolling barrage of their own artillery, but they had no notion of what the jumping-off place looked like. Nevertheless, they pressed on, soaked to the skin, urging the stumbling new men to keep up.

For the American commanders in the field it was a time of frenzy. Bullard, corps commander as yet without a staff, found Harbord and Summerall desperately mimeographing last-minute orders for distribution to their colonels. Harbord did not even know where he would find ammunition reserves. Then one of his aides discovered a dump which had been placed there for the 1st Division, which was six miles away on the left. Harbord took it over for his 2nd Division.

Colonel Paul Malone of the 2nd Division's 23rd Infantry Regiment, who had plugged a French hole beside the Paris road on the night of June 1 and later directed the capture of Vaux, discovered that one of his three battalions was missing. Somehow they were found, and Malone gave the French guides the proper direction and led his men forward. It was now 4:45 and the troops heard the rolling barrage of their own artillery burst with a roar three hundred yards beyond them in the open while they were still in the forest of Retz. Malone pushed his stumbling men forward on the double, and they broke into the open drenched, exhausted, and without machine guns. Using nothing but rifle and bayonet, they swept on, most of their officers falling as they directed the surge. By eight in the morning Doughboys and Marines had captured a mile of strongly held German defenses.

The Big Red One—six miles to the left of the 2nd Division— had an easier start, having reached the jump-off line an hour before the surprise barrage cracked down, but it faced defenses just as tough and had, in addition, to advance over steep, chalky hills. Nevertheless, the 1st Division kept pace with the 2nd, and its veterans and replacements moved relentlessly up the hills behind French tanks, bayoneting German machine gunners and losing many officers and able sergeants whom Pershing had des-

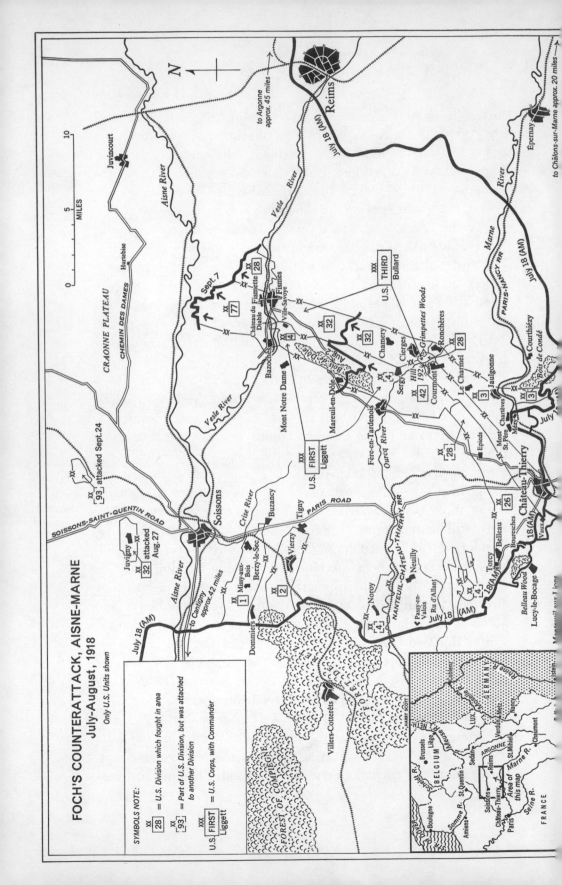

FOCH'S COUNTERATTACK, AISNE-MARNE
July-August, 1918

Only U.S. Units shown

SYMBOLS NOTE:

$\overset{XX}{\boxed{28}}$ = U.S. Division which fought in area

$\overset{XX}{\underset{93}{\boxed{}}}$ = Part of U.S. Division, but was attached to another Division

$\overset{XXX}{\boxed{\text{FIRST}}}$ Liggett = U.S. Corps, with Commander

tined for promotion. By 8 A.M. the Big Red One, too, had advanced a mile into German defenses.

Both divisions now faced a broad plain broken by hills, plateaus, and deep ravines stretching to the valley of the Crise River which flowed northward into the Aisne at Soissons. Without hesitating they continued their attacks, and by ten in the morning the 1st Division held the objective Foch had asked for by the close of the day—the heights above the Crise River from which he could shell Soissons. Fifteen minutes later French artillery, rushing up behind the Yanks, had begun to play upon the railways of the Soissons communications net with French 155's.

At noon on July 18 General Erich Ludendorff, the German Chief of Staff, received the news that Soissons was being shelled by French artillery, and he immediately telephoned General von Boehn—commanding German troops on the Marne—to pull back fast to avoid encirclement. Ludendorff did not know exactly what had happened, but if the Americans had advanced to within artillery range of Soissons, they must be on the verge of a breakthrough. There is no question the German troops southwest of Soissons had been caught flat-footed that morning, and some had broken for the rear in the face of the surprise and ferocity of the assault.

Meanwhile, the Moroccans were trailing, and the 1st Division to the left and the Marine Brigade of the 2nd to the right thinned their lines, spreading across the gap for a mile until each group of American assault teams could hear the others across the death-struck hills. Then both divisions swept on, leaving their flanks naked in their wildcat assaults, pressing their attacks just as fiercely throughout the next day. By nightfall of July 19, the 2nd Division was within sight of the Château-Thierry road, rendering it useless to the Germans. Harbord demanded that his men be relieved, and the French army commander promptly complied. The surviving Doughboys and Marines came back in order, passing many of their dead comrades along the route. In two days the 2nd Division had advanced seven miles, captured three thousand prisoners, seventy-five guns, and sustained about five thousand casualties.

The 1st Division to the left found the going more difficult on the second day and was short of the Château-Thierry road on the eve of the nineteenth. Its lines were now extended on both flanks and everyone was committed to battle, including its engineers and artillerymen, the latter operating at times over open sights. The division pressed on for two more days, college boys leading fragments of regiments, sergeants scraping together remnants of companies. Brigadier General Beaumont Buck, having lost all his field officers, was heading his brigade like a platoon leader in front-line sweeps, waving his tin hat. On the fourth day of the attack and aided by a fresh French division, Buck's brigade took the town of Berzy-le-Sec, cutting the road to Château-Thierry and coming up even with the advance of the 2nd Division. A colonel of the French Foreign Legion who was on the scene and who had seen many years of war sought out Brigadier Buck under fire to say he deemed it an honor to be on the field with such companions. The 1st Division was then relieved. In four days it had lost 7,200 men and taken 3,500 prisoners and 68 guns.

The two great combat divisions had lost over twelve thousand men, half their total strength, but they had punched a hole seven miles deep and six miles wide in the German lines and presented Foch with a great opportunity to trap and capture the German army to the south. Bullard, Harbord, and Summerall—indeed, all the American generals—speculated in their memoirs that if a sufficient number of strong, fresh American divisions had been on the spot to relieve the first two and to keep pushing ahead the result would have been a major defeat for the Germans that would have hastened the end of the war.

Why Foch did not carry out this plan is not known. We do know that his own forces were tired and depleted, and that only a handful of American divisions were available to him in July. He may have not dared to weaken his lines elsewhere to build up his strength for a possible Soissons breakthrough. On the other hand, we know from his strategy in battles after Soissons that Foch's idea of an offensive was to attack all along the front line rather than concentrate strength for a major effort in one sector. This was his plan for the July 18 offensive. Simultaneously with the attack near Soissons, all around the perimeter of the German salient, scores of French divisions and two other American divisions were sent forward at dawn. All the divisions made some progress, but there was not enough strength in any one sector to gain a breakthrough.

After the war General von Boehn, an honorable soldier not given to alibis, said French strategy had made no difference; he had had plenty of men and guns and had been in no hurry to retreat. His actions at the time bear him out, for even the loss of his supply road from Soissons did not seem to bother him. Disregarding Ludendorff's order to get out fast, Boehn delayed as much as possible, built up his defenses on every piece of high ground north of the Marne, determined to tie the French and Americans down to fighting for every foot of the salient. If Boehn could inflict heavy losses on the enemy, Foch might call off the attack.

Everything that General von Boehn planned came to pass—except that Foch never gave up. The offensive launched on July 18 dragged on through August and into September and is now known to history as the Aisne-Marne offensive. It was a long, bloody series of battles that gradually drove the Germans back from the Marne to the Aisne River. Week after week French and American divisions fought their way forward into the German salient, spending a week or more on the front line before being relieved by a fresh division for a few days rest, then returning to combat to replace another tired outfit.

The map on page 80 shows exactly where each American division fought and the terrain it captured within the German salient. As the rest of the German-held area inside the salient was captured by the French, it is obvious that only about twenty-five percent of the fighting was done by the Yanks. Small as this contribution was, it was considerably more than anything the Doughboys of the A.E.F. had done before.

Strategically, then, the seven-week Aisne-Marne offensive was simply a matter of constant forward pressure by French and American divisions that eventually eliminated the German bulge. Tactically, it was a series of almost daily battles, some involving several divisions, others on a much smaller scale and fought by battalions, regiments, or companies. Two of the American divisions involved, the 26th and the 3rd, we have met before. But the real importance of the Aisne-Marne offensive to the A.E.F. was as a training ground for five Doughboy divisions new to the war. In the next chapter we shall see how these newcomers measured up to the test.

Chapter

9

From the Marne to the Aisne

ONLY ONE of the new U.S.
divisions, the 4th, went into action on the first day of Foch's
offensive. The four infantry regiments of the 4th Division leaped
into the open on the west face of the German salient about fifteen
miles south of the 2nd Division (see map, page 80). The men
were pea-green; not one had ever been in combat or even known a
tour of duty in quiet trenches. But they had a first-rate commander
in the lean, unbending Major General George H. Cameron, who
had trained his division of "Regulars," made up mostly of draftees,
at Camp Greene, North Carolina. Because another division had
priority on the target ranges, Cameron had spent eight hours a
day teaching his men to march. When they arrived in France in
May, 1918, they were the best drilled soldiers and the least skilled
marksmen in the A.E.F.

Sent to train in a rear area with the British, Cameron's men
learned about Vickers machine guns and Stokes mortars. They
also discovered that the British had strange names for everything:
to a British Tommie a monkey wrench was a "combination exten-
sion spanner wrench." It was all very puzzling to the Yanks.
Their training was interrupted when they were rushed to the

Marne area as support troops after the German breakthrough on the Chemin des Dames in late May. At this time some of the division's infantrymen had yet to fire a rifle, and others had pistol holsters but no pistols. Cameron offered to relieve the Marines fighting at Belleau Wood with those of his men who had fired a rifle, but Pershing wisely declined. In the next few weeks they learned to master the French weapons, such as the Chauchat, and then they were deemed ready.

The 4th Division did not yet have its own artillery, so its infantry regiments were separated, contrary to Pershing's intentions, and scattered through the II and III Corps of a French army. They attacked due east on the morning of July 18, taking the town of Noroy. Early the next morning one battalion was ordered to take a ravine two miles ahead. H-hour was 4 A.M., and by 5:30 the battalion had captured the ravine. But the French general had changed his timing without passing the word: 5:30 was to be the H-hour to shell the ravine before a "surprise" assault. The battalion now suffered horribly both from the fire of German batteries who knew they had lost the ravine and from the fire of French gunners who did not know the Doughboys had won it. It was the most severe initiation any American unit ever received. Two officers and 93 men were killed, 11 officers and 436 men wounded, one officer and 66 men missing. There were only 609 out of 1,281 able to answer adjutant's call.

One company with fifty-nine men surviving out of two hundred, and one officer out of six, was absolutely helpless to withstand the shock of a possible German counterattack. Suddenly a freckle-faced buck private—and his name is not listed—rounded up the survivors, some of them sergeants, and marched them up to the only officer still on his feet. "Lieutenant, I got about fifty of 'em here. Where'll I put 'em?" The division historian said this nameless boy was made a sergeant.

On the far right, single companies soon fought along with the French. One battalion was so green it left its extra belts of ammunition in bivouac and continued on imperturbably with bayonets when its bullets were exhausted. The French liaison officer reported: "Had I not seen it with my own eyes, I would never have believed green troops would advance under such fire."

It was not until August 2, north of the Ourcq River in the heart of the German salient, that the 4th was allowed to fight as a unified division with its own artillery—and its Doughboys gave a fine account of themselves. When Pershing pulled the division out to rest the third week in August, he considered it a veteran outfit. It had lost 5,486 men while learning the techniques of war and was well trained for future duty.

The 42nd Rainbow Division got into action for nine days, July 25–August 2, south of the Ourcq River (see map, page 80), its assignment to drive the Germans out of chalky hills and woods bristling with machine guns and one-inch cannon. The Rainbows were composed of National Guard elements from many states, unlike the other National Guard divisions, which were organized locally. Just as the 2nd Division had its Doughboy-Leatherneck rivalry of brigades, the Rainbows were capable of competition between regiments and companies. The most recent feud had originated among the iron hills of Anniston, Alabama. There a Manhattan regiment, "The Fighting Sixty-Ninth," composed largely of legendary New York City Irishmen, proved itself expert at night-time chicken stealing during summer maneuvers, to the chagrin of Southern boys in the division who considered chicken stealing their specialty.

"The Fighting Sixty-Ninth" was now known as the 165th U.S. Infantry. Some of its colorful personnel were the principal chaplain, Father Duffy, known as the Vicar of Times Square, and William J. (Wild Bill) Donovan, who would later win the Medal of Honor as a regimental commander, and twenty-five years later, in World War II, would be a two-star general in the Secret Service. The regimental poet was Sergeant Joyce Kilmer, author of the ballad "Trees" so often sung by ladies at chicken salad luncheons. The Rainbows were immensely proud of him.

The division chief of staff was Brigadier General Douglas MacArthur. Even as a brigadier, Douglas MacArthur, with a legendary father who had won the Medal of Honor on Missionary Ridge in the Civil War, was becoming something of a legend himself. The 42nd Division had received its combat indoctrination in support of the French east of Reims following the German assault of July 15. MacArthur's job as chief of staff had been the infinitely difficult one of trying to control the movement of his men as they advanced through French outfits to aid in counterattacks.

The Rainbows had been outstanding in their ferocity during this engagement, and they had learned fast. The Germans knew when the green Americans were facing them and employed various ruses to fight them. One German group came forward in poilu uniforms with friendly calls in French-accented English, and were promptly machine-gunned. Another group tried the ruse in the dark; there was not a shot fired when all twenty-one Germans were met in a friendly fashion—and then bayoneted by the chicken thieves from Wild Bill Donovan's outfit. German prisoners, confused by the large size of the 42nd compared to the size of French and German divisions, had said they were opposing the "two best divisions in the American Army—the 42nd Division and the Rainbow Division."

Father Duffy recalled that when the Doughboys of his joyous Irish regiment learned a few days later that they were to fight in the Champagne country of the German salient, they expected to find bottles of the sparkling wine hanging from every tree. Still, they took over their sector with great savagery, replacing the front of what would have been three French divisions. Their artillery caught everyone's attention for its furiously rapid rate of fire. In two days they cleaned out two miles of German machine guns and cannon in the forested hills east of Fère-en-Tardenois, an important railway town in the center of the salient, and paid copiously with Doughboy blood.

Every man of the 42nd was saddened by the death of their poet, Sergeant Joyce Kilmer. He had asked to go forward with a regimental reconnaissance party on July 30, and a sniper shot him through the forehead. Father Duffy said that the gentle

Kilmer seemed to have the word *fated* written across his brow. The Rainbows buried him beside the Ourcq River, a purling little stream not deep enough to lap into a fisherman's boots.

The Rainbows took many prisoners who were eager to talk to German-speaking Doughboys. Unlike Boehn's well-fed shock troops of the July 15 attack, the Germans taken in the salient were discouraged and ravenous. They dipped their fingers hungrily into cans of corned-beef hash and told the Rainbows, "If there are more like you, then the game is up." They felt they could only fight a delaying action and hope for a decent peace, and they dreaded a long drawn out war.

As the Rainbows swept on, they captured a position whose German enlisted men said they had been compelled to stand alongside their machine guns and field pieces by officers with drawn revolvers. But MacArthur warned the Doughboys that these same fellows, if permitted to withdraw, would fight on with great skill. And so they did; those Germans that were not captured fell back to one strong position after another.

As July waned and the dust of the Champagne country powdered the Doughboys as white as flour millers, Major General Charles H. Muir's Pennsylvanians went into action near the center of the salient (see map, page 80). The division had been in support of the French division to the right of Colonel McAlexander's 38th Infantry Regiment during the German attack of July 15, and four of its companies had seen considerable fighting there. Now General von Boehn's German Seventh Army would know the stupendous shock of the 28th Division's seventeen thousand riflemen and machine gunners fighting as a unit.

The division's diarists were embarrased by the richness of the valor shown by their men. Grimpettes Woods, with seven hundred yards of wheat fields facing it, was like a small-scale Belleau Wood. Two ferocious assaults against the woods were made and repulsed on the morning of July 30 before artillery managed to come up. When the guns arrived at two-thirty that afternoon, the infantry refused to wait for them to get the range.

It charged for the third time and captured the woods with bayonets.

The key to the woods was a church in the village of Courmont, and the Pennsylvanians were shocked because the Germans had turned a House of God into a fort. Doughboys had to use grenades against snipers behind a beautiful altar, batter plaster saints to kill enemy gunners, and fight their way up the stairs to the belfry. Only the sergeant leading the rush survived. He killed the three gunners serving a 77 artillery piece in the belfry and reported that the surviving lieutenant had jumped to his death.

The Pennsylvanians had their share of the miracles attending every war. Lieutenant Stuart Alexander was in a brick building with nineteen other Doughboys and two German prisoners when an eight-inch shell scored a direct hit. Twenty men were killed outright and one was wounded, and Alexander found himself standing on the opposite side of the street, his hair still combed and not a spot on his uniform. Another Doughboy, Private Paul Helsel, returned with the survivors of his company after taking thirty machine guns in the ruins of Château du Diable. Helsel had six bullet holes in his shirt, two in his breeches, and one embedded in his first-aid pack. In the final rush, his bayonet was shot away.

After the Pennsylvanians captured Courmont, Grimpettes, and the terrible Hill 192 behind the woods, they were withdrawn for a well-earned rest. They had proved their worth to Pershing and the French generals, and they would see plenty of action in the battles ahead.

"Tell your men I like their spirit," Pershing had ordered Major General William G. Haan of the 32nd Division when they moved toward the Vesle River (see map, page 80) the last week of July after only twenty-five days of training in Alsace. Pershing had just swooped down from Chaumont to review them. He rode horseback to inspect the artillery and engineers but walked the miles between the ranks of infantry, looking at every button on the blouses of seventeen thousand riflemen and machine gunners. So far, Pershing liked the 32nd's buttons.

The 32nd Division had a proud Civil War record. Its National Guardsmen were composed mainly of Michigan and Wisconsin units, with long records of friendly rivalry. As both states contained many people of German ancestry, many of the 32nd's Doughboys spoke better German than English, though one of their best sergeants was a graduate of Haskell Indian Institute, a Chippewa who stood five-feet-two, weighed 115 pounds, and became noted for his ferocity on patrols. They were a close lot, given to going everywhere together and singing German beer hall songs, yet when they trained near Waco, Texas, the local citizens spoke of them as "Waco's Own." They were the sixth division to arrive in France, February, 1918, and they' nearly had their hearts broken immediately. Someone at Chaumont, not so intelligent as Lieutenant von Buy, thought it best for the sake of security to break up so many German-Americans, and the 32nd's Doughboys were told they would be shipped as individual replacements to other divisions. Fortunately, Pershing countermanded the order as soon as he heard of it.

The German-speaking Doughboys put their language ability to good use on the battlefield, astonishing German prisoners by lecturing to them on the disadvantages of living under Prussian rule. Once, stretcher-bearers bringing a wounded German officer back to Intelligence understood every word as he railed that the pigheaded Americans would lose the war. "Whatever happens, *Herr Oberst*," his bearers said in German as good as his, "you are not going to win anything." And without ceremony they rolled him out to the side of the road.

The men of the 32nd streamed onto the battlefield on August 1 near the village of Cierges, and the French command let them fight their way north twenty miles to Fismes on the Vesle River. Here the Germans were firmly entrenched, and General Mondésir, the French corps commander, went forward to see the American battalions assault the enemy positions. Watching them in action he shuddered and cried, "Yes! Yes! They are terrors!" and turning away, went back to corps headquarters, muttering, "Excellent, excellent."

The Story of the Doughboys

When French General Mangin heard of this, he wanted to use the 32nd to capture the town of Juvigny. Since the 1st and 2nd Divisions had been relieved on July 19–21, Mangin's weary Frenchmen had managed to drive only five miles north of Soissons. There the town of Juvigny, and German gunners in steep, wooded hills, had held them up. So on August 27 and 28, with all its infantry regiments deployed, the 32nd attacked. There were two miles of heavy fighting before the division gave the town to General Mangin at the second sundown. This feat gave the French the road leading north from Soissons to Saint-Quentin. Mangin thanked the men of the 32nd, and in relieving them issued an Army order in which he borrowed General Mondésir's words and referred to the 32nd as "The Terrors."

The fifth new American division to get into Foch's offensive against the German salient was the 77th, composed of New York National Guardsmen. The 77th relieved the 4th north of Bazoches on August 14 (see map, page 80). By this time the salient had been wiped out as far as the Vesle River, but Foch was still driving for the Aisne River more than five miles further north, and the 77th was given its chance to gain some valuable experience in a month of fighting between these two rivers.

The 77th was called the Melting Pot Division, New York City's own. It spoke forty-two languages, and among its numbers could be found Chinese from Mott Street, Jewish boys from Allen Street, Italian boys from east of Union Square. There were Germans from Yorkville on Manhattan's Upper East Side, Turks who spoke a little Hebrew and Hebrews who spoke a bit of Arabic. Many could speak nothing but Brooklyn English; their accent was that of the Don Marquis ballad that ended;

> Prince, when you call on a Brookalyn goil,
> Say Poil for Pearl, and erl for oil.

There were even some Kentucky and Tennessee immigrants to New York City who referred to a dud shell as a "possum playin' daid."

The 77th came into the fighting at its heaviest, going after entrenched enemy positions in the caves above the Vesle River at Fismettes. Their commander, Major General Robert Alexander, understood his New Yorkers. One day when the going was heaviest he issued a general order urging platoon leaders to improve their "gang spirit" to reap the full benefit of the magnificent fighting qualities of the men; and their historian said there were many gangsters among them. They were not easy to con. When Alexander said he would send the enemy two shells to its one, the New Yorkers counted the screams and counter-screams of the French 75s and German 77s passing overhead to see if this two-star bird at headquarters was trying to con them. They decided Alexander was as good as his word.

Typical of the division's diversity were Sergeant Sing Kee and Captain Wardlaw Miles. The sergeant, whose birth had been heralded in proper Chinese style with firecrackers in San Francisco, was one of thirty men operating the message center at the village of Mont Notre Dame. When all twenty-nine of his buddies were knocked out he thought this nothing worth reporting and remained at his post alone for twenty-four hours, all messages coming through. Sergeant Sing was awarded the Distinguished Service Cross.

Captain Miles was a quiet Princeton professor who, in one assault, personally cut the German barbed wire obstructing his company when his own artillery had failed to blast a path through it. As he did so his legs were broken and one arm fractured by machine-gun fire. Nevertheless, once the wire was cut he insisted on being carried forward on a stretcher, and under his direction the attack gained a mile of ground. Later, in a base hospital, he sat quietly and calmly smoking with his free hand while a bevy of doctors and nurses with sponges and probes worked over his painful, multiple wounds. (He never bothered to mention that he had been awarded the Medal of Honor.)

Foch relieved the New Yorkers of the 77th on September 16 after a month of hard fighting. By this time the drive toward the Aisne had taken a back seat to larger and more ambitious plans.

One of these plans, the Saint-Mihiel offensive, was already history; another, the Meuse-Argonne offensive, was just ahead, and it was to be one in which the 77th would play a memorable role.

By the end of August, Foch and Pershing knew they could count on each of these five divisions—the 4th, 42nd, 28th, 32nd, and 77th—for the fighting ahead. Added to the 1st, 2nd, 3rd, and 26th, this meant that the A.E.F. would be able to contribute nine experienced divisions and over 200,000 men to help make up Foch's manpower shortage. And this was only the beginning. All summer long American Doughboys in increasing numbers arrived at French ports and were shipped to training areas. The trickle of U.S. manpower had become a torrent, and everywhere behind the lines Yanks were setting up their own railroad systems and repair shops, telephone and telegraph installations, barracks and hospitals—all the facilities and services necessary to keep a large army in the field. There would shortly be a million American technicians and Doughboys, from stevedores to typists, behind the lines in the Service of Supply. And they would be attending to the needs of a million American fighting men on the front line.

August 1918 was the brightest month for the Allies in four long years of war. In addition to the buildup of American strength and the victories in the Champagne country, on August 8 the British struck a crushing surprise blow against German forces at Amiens, causing heavy losses and a severe shock to German morale. Sensing that the British victory would put Foch in a receptive mood, Pershing visited him on August 9 to get his approval for the formation of an American First Army that would be composed of three corps, each corps containing several divisions. Up to this time there had not been enough American divisions to form an independent American army with its own army commander, which is the way the French, British, and Germans were organized. Elated by the way things were going and encouraged by the fine showing of the Yank divisions since June, Foch granted Pershing's request.

Pershing kept silent for four days and then on August 13, unable to restrain his exultation, he released the news to the American press. Of course, the American First Army's plans were not announced. Yet in Paris the first week in September when Eddie Rickenbacker, America's greatest flying ace of the war, went there on leave, everyone seemed to know. *Les Américains* were going to attack at Saint-Mihiel, and some of the taxi drivers could tick off the numerals of the divisions that were hastening there in the darkness.

Chapter

10

Saint-Mihiel: The Birth of an Army

O<small>N AUGUST</small> 30, a proud General Pershing in command of his American First Army took over the forty-mile front that bounded the Saint-Mihiel salient. The French generals were on hand for the ceremony, clad in their dark blue coats and red breeches. They were glad to be leaving the unpleasant sector, with its dusty summers and swampy winters, and the constant scrutiny of German telescopes on Montsec, the German-held hill that dominated the landscape.

The Germans had captured the city in 1914, extending their hold on its western and southern sides until they formed an L-shaped protrusions into French lines (see map, page 98). The French had lost 125,000 men trying fruitlessly to retake the city in 1915. Since then it had been a comparatively quiet sector while fierce battles had raged at Verdun and on the Somme and Flanders fronts, but the French longed to win it back.

Foch and Pershing had agreed that the American First Army would attack and capture Saint-Mihiel. Once this was accomplished, Pershing planned to push northeast into Germany toward the German city of Metz and the important Briey iron mines. But no sooner had Pershing taken over command of the sector than he received a visit from Foch, who brought with him entirely new plans. The new American army would be split up into two halves, and both halves would join two separate French armies west of Verdun and fight under French generals. Pershing was furious, but after a spirited argument lasting several days both men compromised. The American First Army would not be split up, but Pershing would fight where Foch wanted.

What followed was one of the most difficult undertakings in the history of war, for Foch ordered the Americans to reduce the Saint-Mihiel salient and, immediately afterward, to move sixty miles north and open an offensive in the Meuse-Argonne sector. The date set for the attack on Saint-Mihiel was September 12; the date decided on for the Meuse-Argonne offensive was September 26. In Pershing's words, "We had undertaken to launch, with the same army . . . two great attacks on battlefields sixty miles apart." Both attacks would have to take place within a period of two weeks.

During the weeks of preparation for the Saint-Mihiel attack, American intelligence decided to play a few tricks to confuse the Germans. Doughboy divisions east of the salient at Belfort were ordered to send out reconnaissance parties as though in preparation for an attack, and their radio stations made the nights crackle with coded messages. Tanks were sent out at night to make misleading tracks for German aviators to photograph in the daytime. Finally, Colonel A. C. Conger of Pershing's General Staff, a famous trouble-shooter, arrived in Belfort and engaged a room in the best hotel. Sitting down at his writing desk he took two sheets of paper and a fresh sheet of carbon paper and made out a one-page report in duplicate to Pershing on the status of the imaginary attack at Belfort. He then sent both the original and duplicate off by courier, balled the carbon paper into a tight wad, tossed it into the wastebasket, and went down to the bar for a five-minute drink. Spies were everywhere in Belfort; the Swiss

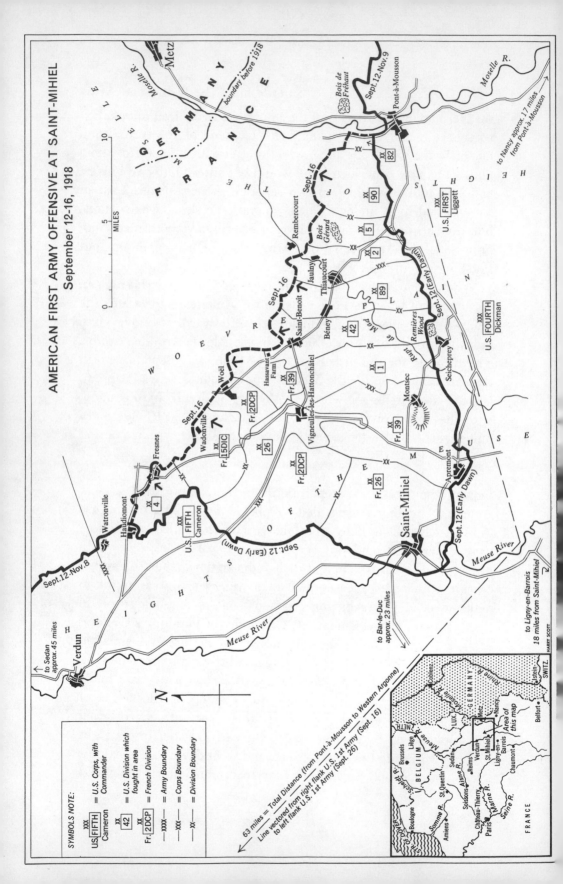

AMERICAN FIRST ARMY OFFENSIVE AT SAINT-MIHIEL
September 12-16, 1918

MILES

SYMBOLS NOTE:

US|FIFTH|Cameron = U.S. Corps, with Commander

XX 42 = U.S. Division which fought in area

Fr. 2DCP = French Division

———— = Army Boundary

——— = Corps Boundary

—— = Division Boundary

63 miles = Total Distance (from Pont-à-Mousson to Western Argonne)
Line vectored from right flank U.S. 1st Army (Sept. 16)
to left flank U.S. 1st Army (Sept. 26)

HARRY SCOTT

border and the active espionage market in Geneva were just a short distance away. So Conger was not surprised on returning to his room to find his wastebasket empty.

The result of these ruses was that the Germans evacuated some hospitals and villages near Belfort, moved up additional artillery, and brought up three divisions as reserves. They did not, however, shift any of their forces from Saint-Mihiel to Belfort.

In making his plans for the offensive, Pershing chose to confine his main blows to the south face of the salient, with a converging attack by one division from the west. There would be two American corps on the south face, the Ist and IVth, plus the French 3rd (Colonial) Corps at the nose of the angle nearest the city itself. The third American corps, the Vth, would be on the west face of the salient.

Each American corps contained a mixture of experienced divisions and outfits that had just finished their training. In all, there would be nine Doughboy divisions and four French divisions taking part in the attack. The corps commanders were Major General Joseph T. Dickman for the IVth Corps, Major General George H. Cameron for the Vth Corps, and Major General Hunter Liggett for the Ist Corps. Dickman and Cameron had earned their promotions leading the 3rd and 4th Divisions, respectively, during the fighting of July and August between the Marne and Aisne rivers. Liggett was Pershing's best general and was the first American assigned command of a corps. At the time of Foch's July 18 offensive and in the weeks that followed he had led a corps of Doughboy and French divisions, serving under a French army commander. The rumor was that he owed his high position that July 18 to his fall from a horse.

Liggett had arrived in France in March, 1918, and was subjected to the merciless scrutiny Pershing gave all his generals— a searching character analysis as well as a medical survey to determine if they were fit to command troops in the field. Liggett brought with him a brilliant record in the peacetime army and a reputation as a tactical wizard, but he was very fat. "I have no fat above my collar," he is reputed to have told Pershing. Yet

Pershing must have wondered how Liggett could make the twice-weekly tour of the front line that Pershing demanded, with all that crawling around in dugouts and shell holes. Liggett began violent horseback exercises in the hope of reducing, and on one strenuous gallop he was catapulted into a bone-shaking fall. His fellow riders held their breath, fearing the general might explode, and someone rode off for an ambulance. But before anyone could dismount to attend him, Liggett was up and on his horse. This agility was reported to Pershing and, so the story goes, convinced him that Liggett was not too fat to fight.

Pershing's new army was going to have excellent support for the Saint-Mihiel attack. The French supplied 267 light tanks, 3,020 pieces of artillery of all calibers, and the French Air Division of some six hundred planes. The British sent the best air arm then in being, the Independent Bombing Squadrons of the Royal Air Force. Together with the new Aviation Section of the U.S. Signal Corps, Pershing had about thirteen hundred airplanes.

The Yanks had two innovations: giant-sized, two-handed, barbed-wire clippers of Spanish-American War vintage, and rolls of chicken wire eighteen feet in length to be thrown as footpaths over any barbed wire that was left uncut. The French were fascinated by the chicken wire, and General Pétain sent captains and sergeants to study it; but poilu officers reported it was useful only to Doughboys, who had long legs and big feet.

Colonel George C. Marshall, Jr., who had been chief of staff of the 1st Division during the Cantigny attack, was now an intelligence officer on Pershing's staff. After studying the formidable German defenses of deep dugouts, permanent installations and broad belts of barbed wire built up over a four-year period, Marshall recommended a fourteen-hour artillery bombardment prior to the attack. However, Pershing settled for four hours of preliminary shelling, hoping this would be enough to soften German strongpoints and still not give them time to bring up reinforcements.

By coincidence, the Germans had planned to shorten their exposed front lines by pulling back on September 12. They had begun their withdrawal before dawn that morning when the American bombardment began, forcing them underground. The 1st U.S. Gas Regiment gave the divisions attacking the south face of the salient forty minutes of smoke screen, enabling all Doughboys to reach their jump-off lines without molestation. By the time the bombardment lifted, Doughboys were chucking grenades into dugouts, and the German inhabitants were hurrying to get out with hands up. Everything went smoothly as the new 5th, 82nd, 89th, and 90th Divisions drove north, receiving their baptism of fire in offensive warfare. (The "Texas Brigade" of the 90th was led by Ulysses Grant McAlexander, who had won his brigadier general's star and, as usual, reached his objective with the advance patrols.) The veteran 1st, 2nd, and 42nd Divisions drove forward with ease, for the only time in the war sustaining just a few casualties.

The Saint-Mihiel salient was eliminated when the 26th Division, pushing southeast from the west face, met the northbound 1st Division at the village of Hattonchâtel in the heart of the salient at sunrise September 13, after both outfits had pushed on all night. It had been a remarkably quick and easy victory. General von Fuchs, the German commander on the field, was scolded by his superiors for the unexpected beating his divisions received. He continued feeble resistance until September 16, when the Doughboys entrenched on the new line, now virtually straight from Haudiomont to Pont-à-Mousson (see map, page 98). Fuchs had given up sixteen thousand prisoners and 450 cannon. American casualties were seven thousand, one third of Medical Corps expectations, which had brought up sixty hospital trains and prepared fifteen thousand beds for casualties from the south face of the salient alone.

Historians rightly look upon Saint-Mihiel not as a difficult victory but as an example of a large-scale offensive carried out with surprise and skill. It was a great morale booster to the French. Pershing always felt it did more to revive the French than the stand at the Marne by the 3rd Division on July 15, or the more bloody victories between the Marne and the Aisne, or even the great British victory at Amiens. It was far more prominently played up in the French press than these other victories, and even Premier Clemenceau, the Tiger of France, and President Poincaré came up to Saint-Mihiel to offer congratulations.

President Poincaré had recently awarded Pershing the Legion of Honor, and had had great difficulty bestowing the traditional French accolade of a kiss on each cheek that was customary on such occasions. The ex-plowboy from the Missouri cornfields stood six feet tall in his boots. Monsieur Poincaré was five-feet-four in his pointed French shoes. The President and Mme. Poincaré also visited their modest home in Saint-Mihiel and found it a mass of rubble, blown to bits by vindictive German gunners before they were captured. Witnesses reported that the French President, looking at the shards of his residence, simply said, *"C'est la guerre,"* and turned away dry-eyed.

11

The Meuse-Argonne: Opening Day

In SEPTEMBER 25's night sky above the Argonne Forest, a German aviator cut his engine and listened, gliding silently just above treetop level. He could see no lights below, but he could hear the bellow of mule skinners, the shouts of drill sergeants, the racket of light tank engines, and the crashing of truck gears. In daylight, there would have been little to photograph because of the concealing treetops, but there was no mistaking the bedlam. *The Yanks were coming*.

The ultimate goal of the planned American offensive was the French city of Sedan, captured by the Germans in the first month of the war. Ever since, it had become an important German railway hub through which they supplied their armies in the west. The ten miles of track from Sedan to Mézières was the Germans' jugular vein, and in the American First Army Pershing had just the weapon to slit it. North of Sedan was the Ardennes region of Belgium, mountainous, forested, and nearly impassable in winter, which was just a few months away. The American attack was to be coordinated with a British drive due east from their positions

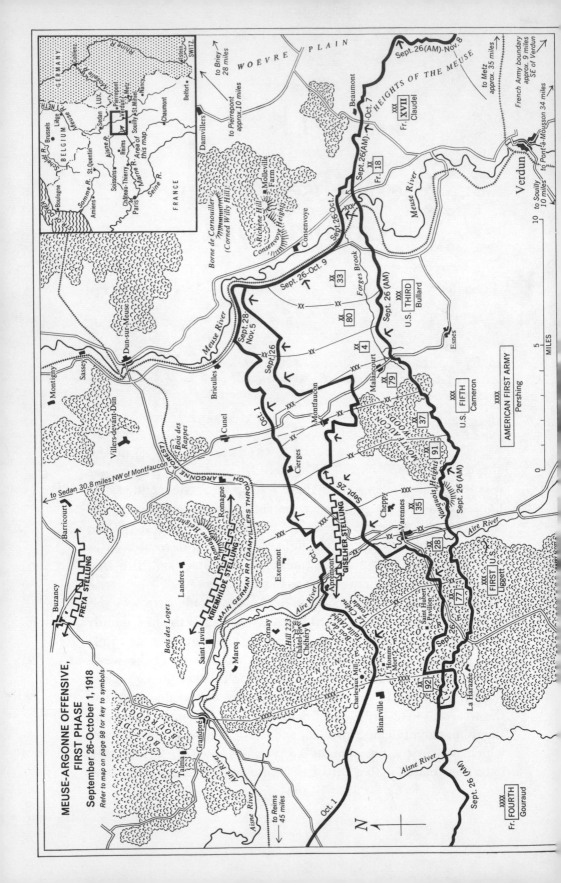

MEUSE-ARGONNE OFFENSIVE, FIRST PHASE
September 26-October 1, 1918

Refer to map on page 98 for key to symbols.

to the northwest, and a French assault due north through the valley of the Aisne River on the American left flank. If the Americans could take Sedan and cut the railway lifeline to Germany, the German armies would be trapped between the French, British, and American forces.

The shortest route to Sedan for the Doughboys ran due north from where the Reims-Verdun front line crossed the north-flowing Aisne and Aire rivers, with the Argonne Forest between them. Pershing, for once given a choice of route, if not ultimate goal (he would still have preferred Metz), chose to open his attack through the valley of the Aire rather than the Aisne, with the Argonne Forest on his left flank, the north-flowing Meuse River on his right. The American First Army front also ran several miles east of the Meuse, but this was difficult, mountainous country, and the main attack was to take place west of the river, where 225,000 Doughboys in three full corps, each corps with three divisions, were to push north on a twenty-five-mile front.

If the Meuse-Argonne front was the shortest route to Sedan, it was still forty miles, and the first fifteen were a nightmare. The primary obstacle was the country itself. The Argonne was ten miles of dense forest growth, rocky slopes, cliffs, ravines, innumerable brooks; its surface was shellholed and appeared as desolate as the moon. The course of the Aire River was just as difficult. It twisted north about fifteen miles, then turned west above the forest at the village of Grandpré to join the Aisne. The valley of the Aire presented the extra hazard of open spaces offering no cover for the attackers. Further east was the towering hill of Montfaucon, from whose crest the Germans could direct artillery fire all over American lines, and along the east bank of the Meuse were the imposing hills known as the Heights of the Meuse.

The Germans had had four years to improve the natural difficulty of the terrain with carefully built defenses. They had also constructed a formidable line behind the front just in case they were thrown back. Named after the German field marshal, Paul von Hindenburg, the Hindenburg Line stretched more than a hundred miles from west to east, a network of barbed wire, trenches, machine-gun emplacements, and concrete shelters averaging seven miles in depth. In the Meuse-Argonne sector the line was particularly strong because of its proximity to Verdun, the famous city that the French and Germans had fought over since 1915, with combined losses of more than a million men.

Facing the Americans on September 26 was the First Position, mainly barbed wire and machine-gun units. Three miles behind it was the Intermediate Position, studded with cannon and fortified in depth from the Aisne River to the forts on the Heights of the Meuse. Behind this outlying complex was the first of the three main Hindenburg barriers—the Giselher Stellung (or Fortress), with the tall hill of Montfaucon in the center. Five miles to the rear was the second barrier, the Kriemhilde Stellung, built along the ridges of the Romagne Heights. The last-ditch barrier was another five miles away, built on the bristling hills around the village of Buzancy. It was called the Freya Stellung. The German defenders, four-year professionals, had named their three strongly fortified barriers after witches from the operas of Richard Wagner.

The Germans had built comfortable dugouts and bombproofs, libraries and clubhouses, and they were able to wage almost push-button warfare. Every road and bridge, every possible avenue of attack had been studied, its distance and range recorded in advance for artillery fire from three directions. The Germans had inflicted shocking losses on the French poilus when the latter had attempted to dislodge them in 1915, and they did not expect another attack by the ignorant Americans to succeed any better. The Germans planned to go underground when the American shelling began, taking their newspapers, scientific journals, pipes, and knitting needles with them. When in the dawn the shelling ceased and the first Doughboy began to claw at the first strands of wire, the Germans would be ready to meet him with all their accomplished deviltry. Secure in their four-year fastness, the

Germans knew better than anyone the amount of effort it would take to drive them back.

As soon as Foch and Pershing had agreed in early September that the Meuse-Argonne sector would follow Saint-Mihiel as the next target for the American First Army, Pershing's staff began making preparations. There were 3,980 guns of all calibers that had to be in place by September 25, plus 40,000 tons of shells. Once the firing began, fourteen trainloads of shells would be needed daily, arriving from twenty-four ammunition depots established at nineteen railheads. Quartermasters and engineers would require twenty-nine more depots, Chemical Warfare six, and trucks would need nine depots for gasoline and oil. Forage would have to be brought up for ninety-thousand mules and horses, and surgeons would need thirty-four evacuation hospitals. Engineers had to rebuild 164 miles of light railways, and sixty-five miles of standard track. It was a tremendous task on such short notice, but by the night of September 25 everything was ready; all of the nine divisions assigned to the first day's assault were in line, and Pershing was able to issue his battle orders.

On the eve of this historic moment, the launching of the biggest coordinated Allied offensive of the war, and, it was hoped, the final attack that would bring victory, Foch was at his new Supreme Command Headquarters in the deserted town of Bombon. Colonel T. Bentley Mott, Pershing's official representative at French Headquarters, met him on the street. Foch's gilt-encrusted cap was cocked over his right ear, his back ramrod stiff, his barrel-stave legs fairly prancing as he walked along swinging his swagger stick. As Mott braced and saluted the most famous Allied soldier in the world, the marshal stopped and eyed him. Mott knew that being stared at by Foch, a man of few words, was an invitation to speak. The colonel mumbled something about how things were going rather well, weren't they? Foch's reply was in pantomime, and it was prophetic. He seized Mott's belt with his left hand, dug a right fist into Mott's ribs, clipped him with a cross to the chin, then a blow to the ear. Having demonstrated his victory combinations, the old fighter cock-a-hooped on without a word, carrying his stick at shoulder arms.

There was an aerial witness to the opening moments of the Meuse-Argonne offensive. Captain Eddie Rickenbacker, the great American ace, took off before dawn on a sortie behind German lines. As he flew north through the blackness over the front he looked down and saw flashes that reminded him of a switchboard in a giant telephone exchange—the great artillery bombardment preceding the infantry assault. On his return it was daylight, and through the haze and smoke he could see some ants swarming on molehills—Doughboys in open patches assaulting fortified knolls. Having lived close to fiery death in the sky, Rickenbacker wondered why those ants on the ground "did not go absolutely mad with terror."

As the infantry of nine American divisions moved forward at 5:30, Ligget's I Corps on the left sent the New Yorkers of the 77th Division into the depths of the Argonne Forest. Only recently relieved from fighting against General von Boehn in the Aisne-Marne sector, the 77th was a sleepless, unrested outfit, and by now it was below full strength.

Nevertheless, the New Yorkers, with the French on their left, made a brilliant rush that first day, slipping forward through the tangle of forest, hidden from the Germans until their forward patrols came into the sight rings of Spandau machine guns. By evening all four infantry regiments were widely deployed three miles from their jump-off points. But the day had worn them out, and the 77th's Doughboys faced formidable obstacles on the morrow.

Liggett's center division was the now veteran 28th of Pennsylvania National Guardsmen under General Muir. This division, too, was exhausted from constant fighting. Only one third of its men were protected by the trees of the Argonne. The other two thirds were exposed to German fire from the hills on either side of the valley of the Aire River (see map, page 104). Facing the Pennsylvanians were massive belts of barbed wire that no amount of artillery fire could have blasted. The infantry went forward at 5:30 and was through the wire by 9 o'clock in the morning, much Pennsylvania blood and flesh clinging to the rusty barbs, only to find themselves shelled and machine-gunned from the heights beyond. Had there been a thousand guns to back them up, and three hundred heavy tanks to clean out the banks of the Aire, they might have succeeded. As it was, they tried again and again in assaults on these cliffs with their countless guns, and they suffered horribly.

There were many such lads as Corporal Donald M. Call, a tank driver whose tank turret was torn off by a shell burst. He crawled out and found a fine, muddy shell hole twenty yards away, then discovered his lieutenant, wounded, was still in the tank. He went back and carried the young officer to the muddy shell hole's comforts, while a battery of field guns sniped at him. It was only a foretaste of the conduct of many Pennsylvanians in the twelve days that would be required to clear all German guns off the heights.

Liggett's right flank division was the new 35th of the Kansas and Missouri National Guard, and no Yank division anywhere ever had a rougher baptism or assignment. Its first obstacle was the Vauquois Heights on the Germans' main Line of Resistance (see map, page 104). The men of the 35th were easily seen by German defenders on the heights and were shelled as they scrambled through a maze of trenches toward their goal. They made three ferocious attacks in the ten hours of daylight that first day over ground that was tunneled and cratered by mines and counter-mining operations.

Private Nels Wold, a Chauchat gunner, and his ammunition carrier got four machine guns that afternoon; when his companion was wounded, Wold fetched him back to shelter, then proceeded alone against the fifth gun of the cluster until his luck ran out. The state of Missouri erected a monument near the Vauquois Heights to such Medal of Honor winners as Private Wold and to hundreds of other Doughboys who fell on this battlefield.

Cameron's three untested divisions, made up mainly of draftees and "ninety-day wonders"—officers with only three months training—formed the V Corps in the center of the American First Army line. All three divisions shared the same assignment, the capture of the lofty hill of Montfaucon (see map, page 104). The plan was for the 91st Division to move forward on the left and the 79th Division on the right, hoping to pinch the defenders of Montfaucon on each flank so that they would be compelled to fall back before a direct assault by the 37th National Guard Division in the center. It was such a difficult assignment that French General Pétain, who knew the ground from his past experience as commander at nearby Verdun, said Montfaucon's capture would be a triumph if it happened by Christmas. But Cameron's lads set to, with a will born of ignorance and idealism, at 5:30 that morning, breaking through the wire on their front and disappearing into the five-mile belt of saplings and thickets of Montfaucon Wood between them and the hill.

Colonel George S. Patton, Jr., destined to be one of the outstanding generals of World War II, was given the honor of leading the 1st Tank Brigade, consisting of light French machines, in the frontal assault of the 37th Division. These little beetles were priority targets for German gunners, and Patton's lead tank was soon disabled along with most of the others. As Patton climbed out of his tank and went after some machine-gun nests on foot, the Germans got their first sight of the man whose irregular but spectacular dress would become legend in the next war. The colonel descended on them with a blazing ivory-handled pistol in each hand, shod in glossy cavalry boots, sporting a gleaming buckle on a spotless Sam Browne belt, with every button of his immaculate uniform brassed to a high luster. He was about as inconspicuous as a diamondback rattlesnake on a green velvet rug, and he was soon being carted back on a stretcher to Headquarters, where Pershing told him his conduct merited the Distinguished Service Cross.

The Germans put up fierce resistance to Cameron's V Corps, for no one knew better than they the value of Montfaucon's elevation. But nothing could stop the rush of the three divisions, and by nightfall Doughboys of the 37th had burst out of the woods and were crouched beneath the mountain's frowning guns. Men dug into the sides of its ravines, seeking any protection from the all-night shelling, ears pricked for the ker-plop of gas shells. It began to drizzle, and the rainy blackness was illuminated by the glare of bursting shells that revealed Doughboys struggling like pack mules under shoulder-loads of food and cartridges. Here and there some hardy mess sergeant wrestled with his rolling kitchens among artillery moving up, hoping to give his rain-soaked buddies, all 25,000 of them without blankets, some hot coffee.

Bullard's III Corps on the right of the American First Army line had different terrain to contend with—low country laced with swamps and brooks—but its problems were no easier. On his ex-treme right next to the Meuse was the 33rd Division, mainly corn-belt National Guardsmen from Illinois, who had had a taste of combat while supporting the British at Amiens in August.

The German defenders along the Meuse were under orders not to give up ground under any conditions, yet the 33rd Division's infantry was through the first line by nine o'clock. Then, as planned, the Illinois men wheeled ninety degrees right to seize and hold the banks of the Meuse, reaching their assigned positions by noon (see map, page 104). By nightfall they had around fif-teen hundred prisoners with all their arms and supplies, and were particularly happy over the capture of a narrow-gauge railway complete with a cheeping locomotive and supply depots. The cost had been remarkably low: fewer than fifty killed and 250 wounded.

Among the 33rd's heroes that first day was Captain George H. Mallon, a giant of a man with a bristling mustache who could eat a six-pound porterhouse steak for breakfast. The mist clung so heavily to the ground he could see only nine of his men. Undeter-red, he captured nine machine guns, taking one when his pistol was empty by knocking the last German gunner cold with a right to the jaw. Moving on, Mallon and his nine men collected an antiaircraft gun and closed on the rear of a German battery of 150 howitzers, taking all four with their astonished crews. Not one of Captain Mallon's Doughboys was wounded in the exploit.

Bullard's center division had never known a day's rehearsal with artillery, an example of one of the drawbacks of this hasty, impromptu offensive, but few of its men needed instruction in the use of the rifle. The 80th Division was composed of squirrel- and possum-hunting marksmen from the Blue Ridge country of Virginia, West Virginia, and Pennsylvania. Some of the men had to learn their three R's in training camp. "I done learned to write," said one of them, dictating a letter home to a Red Cross worker, "but I ain't learned yet to read what I wrote."

The 80th's target for September 26 was the town of Brieulles in the bend of the Meuse six miles due north (see map, page 104). The possum-hunting infantry slogged through the marshes in front of them and were in the first belt of woods beyond by noon. The timetable called for them to attack again at three o'clock, and the Blue Ridge men went forward as scheduled with their rifles, unsupported by artillery, making the woods echo with rebel yells that would have made their southern ancestors proud.

But the Germans were determined to hold Brieulles, and they had the artillery to do it. From towering Montfaucon in the west and the high domes of the Consenvoye Heights and the Borne de Cornouiller ("Corned Willy Hill") east of the Meuse, massed German artillery began to zero in on the exposed men of the 80th during the afternoon assault, and Bullard wisely halted them. It was a tribute to their woodsmanship that their casualties, in spite of this hellish shelling, were only around a thousand men, and that they captured nearly that many prisoners. They had accounted for numberless German snipers in trees, an easy target for squirrel-hunters.

Bullard's third division was the veteran 4th, whose men had hardly had a chance to draw a quiet breath since they jumped off in regimental strength on the first day of Foch's July 18 offensive against the Marne salient. They had seen action as the northernmost division in the Saint-Mihiel attack of September 12, and now they were pushing forward to the left of the 80th Division.

The 4th's tired Doughboys had to fight for each foot of ground the moment the American First Army's heavy guns stopped their preparatory bombardment and the French 75s began dropping their rolling barrage of shells ahead of them. Enemy outposts quickened the air with the chatter of machine guns as khaki-clad groups came out of the smoke. Bullard estimated that German artillery sent them five thousand shells that first day.

The 4th Division proceeded five miles on September 26, breaking through the Line of Resistance protecting the first Stellung of the Hindenburg positions (see map, page 104). But like the 80th on its right flank, when night fell the 4th's survivors were forced to dig in and hold what they had taken. In the·days ahead the 4th Division, as well as the others in Bullard's III Corps, would consider five miles a huge success, and five thousand enemy shells a day a mere pittance.

"The assault of September 26," wrote Pershing after the war, "surprised the Germans and disrupted their defenses, but this situation was only momentary." Montfaucon had been the key to this first day. If it had fallen, it is possible the Doughboys would have pushed beyond the Romagne Heights to breach the Kriemhilde Stellung, the second line of the Hindenburg defense system. Green troops, for the most part, had given the Yanks a heroic first round, but they had not been able to score the breakthrough Pershing and Foch had hoped for. If the veterans of the 1st, 2nd, 3rd, and 42nd Divisions had been able to come up from Saint-Mihiel in time to attack the German center in the Meuse-Argonne sector that first morning, it is possible that Montfaucon would have fallen. As it was, the Doughboys had smashed through from three to five miles of the toughest defenses in Europe, and the knowledgeable Pétain thought the American First Army's achievement that first day was tremendous.

The opening of the Meuse-Argonne offensive marked the beginning of the end. For the next six weeks the American First Army continued to smash ahead in a long series of bloody frontal assaults, slowly driving the Germans back to Sedan. As we shall see, American divisions made contributions on other parts of the front during these weeks, "on loan" to British or French generals. But the Meuse-Argonne offensive was an all-American show, and we shall return to cover its highlights in later chapters.

Chapter

12

Flying the Flaming Coffins

◆

SEPTEMBER 26, the first morning of the Meuse-Argonne offensive, was memorable for another American outfit, one that took to the sky at dawn only a few hours after the lonely Captain Eddie Rickenbacker in his Spad. While Rickenbacker was returning from his sortie behind the front, Colonel William ("Billy") Mitchell, also flying a Spad, was taking off from a French field as leader of a bombing group composed of eight de Haviland 4s, the only American plane used in France. The executive of the bomber group was First Lieutenant Merian C. Cooper, and their orders were to bomb some German supply depots well behind the lines.

Normally Cooper would have been lead pilot in the bomber formation, but his Liberty engine began missing along the taxi strip and he had to let the other planes go by. When Cooper's engine finally caught, he took off after the others and had to full-throttle to join up in the rear position as Tail-End Charlie. Only seven of the eight de Havilands climbed aloft, one plane crashing on the strip, killing both pilot and observer.

In place of Cooper, Lieutenant Sidney Howard, later a Pulitzer Prize playwright, led the way in what he called "the very worst airplane between the North Sea and the Swiss border." The two-seater de Haviland was known as the "flaming coffin" for it was the most vulnerable airplane ever built. The gas tank was located in the fuselage between the open cockpits of pilot and observer, and its Liberty engine was a product of hasty wartime improvisation. An incendiary bullet into its gas tank would create a bonfire between its two occupants, while a tracer into the twelve-cylinder, V-type plant usually set the engine afire. However, any new engine has a hundred bugs, and it is a credit to American industry that the Liberty turned out as well as it did.

By the time the Doughboys were fighting on the Meuse-Argonne front in September of 1918, the Franco-British aviators had won the air with the French Spads and the British Sopwith Camels. Yank infantrymen were never subjected to the horrors of aerial ground strafing, when sometimes whole divisions were broken and dispersed by savagery from the skies.

It had been a costly victory. In fact, most of the great aces of both sides were gone by 1918, but their names and feats were still remembered. The nineteen-year-old Captain Albert Ball of the Royal Flying Corps, a Sunday school boy who had done so much to give the English foot-sloggers in Flanders security from air attack, had forty-three victories before he was shot down in May, 1917. He had made a habit, when returning from German skies, of buzzing a Flemish village to read the hands of the clock on the church tower. Some German Intelligence officer, noting the custom, got Ball with a machine gun secretly placed in the belfry. (Baron von Richthofen, the great German ace, tried to claim that his brother, Lothar von Richthofen, shot Ball down.)

Captain George Guynemer, tubercular hero of French skies with fifty-three well-confirmed victories to his credit, disappeared forever over Flanders September 11, 1917. Again the Germans tried to claim credit, but the chances are Guynemer's lungs had hemorrhaged and he had fainted, crashing unconscious to the ground.

German Captain Werner Voss, "the greatest pilot any of us ever encountered"—according to Captain James McCudden of the Royal Flying Corps, no amateur himself with fifty-eight confirmed victories before he was killed by engine failure on take-off—died on September 23, 1917. The German-Jewish genius dove his red-and-white checkered triplane straight into a twenty-plane mass of British SE-5s, and for twenty minutes kept the wheel of fortune spinning in his favor, with his plane as the axle in a wheel of enemy aircraft, until Lieutenant Albert Rhys-Davids, a nineteen-year-old like Voss, shot him down.

The legendary Richthofen was killed in the spring of 1918. Richthofen was a great birdman, though his claim of eighty victories, inflated by himself and the Kaiser, does not bear postwar examination. However, it was as a strategist and tactician of aerial warfare that Richthofen proved his real greatness as an innovator and leader. Although he was reportedly shot down and killed by a British pilot, there are some who believe he made a successful crash landing in no-man's-land only to be shot through the head by a British sniper. Richthofen was not popular with English and French pilots, as were Voss and most of the other German flyers, because of his Prussian haughtiness and his many untruthful claims. "I hope he roasted all the way down," said Major Edward Mannock, the great English ace with seventy-three victories to his credit, when apprised of Richthofen's death. Mannock himself was killed a few days later in his twenty-first year.

There were others who survived to protect the Doughboys as 1918 drew to a close: Captain René Fonck, highest French scorer with seventy-five victories; Captain William Bishop, the Canadian with seventy victories who never wasted a shot. And by the time of the Meuse-Argonne there were some legendary American pilots, too, in addition to Rickenbacker.

At the beginning of the war American aviators had enlisted in the French Air Squadron, which became the Lafayette Escadrille, and some thirty-eight of them transferred to the Aviation Section of the U.S. Signal Corps after the United States entered the war. At that time these thirty-eight American pilots and fifty-five planes (nearly all obsolete) constituted America's air power. American aviators were trained in France and England under French and British instructors with the help of the men from the Lafayette, and they flew French and British planes, since their own country was only beginning to produce the "Flaming Coffin." Their presence began to be felt during the summer of 1918 over Belleau Wood and the Marne salient, where the courageous young Quentin Roosevelt met his death.

American airpower did not really come into its own until Saint-Mihiel, simultaneously with the debut of the American First Army. In the skies over the salient that week in September some brilliant American flyers met their deaths, and some new legends were born. The popular Major Raoul Lufbery from the Lafayette Escadrille had jumped from his fiery plane near Pont-à-Mousson, trying to hurl his flaming body into a lake. And above a body of water known to aviators as Three Finger Lake the finest feat of any American flyer was performed September 18. If Lufbery was the best loved pilot in the A.E.F. and the shrewd Rickenbacker the highest scorer, Lieutenant Frank Luke, the Arizona Balloon Buster, was the bravest and most admired. He was an unbridled boy, as wild as a Comanche mustang when he took to the sky. Attempts to discipline him were fruitless; frequently he would land on a French field and spend the night there after some fabulous piece of recklessness, fearing he might be grounded for impudence if he returned to his home field. His hatred of enemy observation balloons because of the artillery fire they might direct on the Doughboys was a consuming passion.

Above Three Finger Lake on September 18 Luke set out alone to destroy two German gas bags. Approach was always perilous; the balloon company was surrounded by skillful machine gunners and antiaircraft cannon, often with pursuit planes hiding in ambush in the sun. Sometimes a balloon failed to ignite because the velocity of a tracer bullet was so high it might pass through the bag harmlessly. Luke destroyed his first balloon on his first pass and was immediately aware of three enemy aircraft hovering beyond, waiting for him. He went for them head on, shooting down two Fokkers, while the third airplane took evasive action. When Luke turned to pursue it he realized that by changing course slightly he could make a pass at the second balloon. This he did, shooting it down in flames. He then pursued and destroyed the third German airplane, an observation craft, though he could have left it for six American Spads who were moving toward it.

Luke was a golden boy, with an unequaled record of fourteen victories in eight days, with five victories in eight minutes. The gods loved him, and he did not have to die young. Wounded and downed behind German lines, he could have let himself be captured and he might have sat out the last few weeks of the war in safety. Instead, Luke had leaped out of his cockpit and with his Colt .45 shot it out with a patrol seeking to take him prisoner, dying with his boots on, Western style.

Sidney Howard, Merian Cooper, and the Doughboy infantrymen had many obligations to such as these, French, British, and American, living and dead, who preceded them. But both Howard, leading the flight on September 26 over the Meuse-Argonne, and Cooper, flying rear guard, were too busy to be dwelling on the past. For one thing, they were among the first Americans to cross the lines in a home product, and neither of them had had any experience with bombers, having been trained in two-seater fighters.

The seven airplanes of Howard's and Cooper's flight had just bombed the target and had turned for home when five yellow-and-black Fokkers, sharks of the ocean sky, knifed into them. One Fokker spun out to death below, the others flew off. Unknown to the other six American pilots, the observer in Howard's leading plane had been killed in the encounter, his death throes causing his legs to stretch outward and jam Howard's controls.

Presently, the Yanks saw a flight of Fokkers, sixteen or twenty, alerted by the first encounter, coming at them head on. Normally, such overpowering enemy superiority would have caused the American flight to turn at full throttle and try to get back to home base by way of another route. But with Howard's controls jammed, he could fly only straight ahead, and the other Americans followed. The Fokkers flew in among them, and the sky became garish with the flash of many colors, red and yellow and black paint, streams of tracers, bundles of bonfires, as friend and enemy plummeted in acrobatic pinwheels. It became impossible to distinguish casualties. Howard thought he saw his wing man and best friend, Phil Rhinelander, with his observer, spinning down to cremation. Cooper saw one Yank observer, his machine gun's ammunition gone, stand in the cockpit and throw the gun's steel drum at a Fooker twenty feet away.

Howard, his controls still jammed by his dead observer, flew straight on, followed by Lieutenant Clarkson Potter protecting his rear, both planes miraculously untouched. After proceeding some twenty miles over enemy country, rigor mortis caused Howard's observer to change his posture, and the controls were freed. Howard then made his way back to American lines, leading the faithful Potter, who only had a few days left to live, and Potter's observer, to a French landing field. Only three men of the sixteen who set out that morning made it back alive.

It was months before "Tail-End-Charlie" Cooper's fate was known, at which time he wrote a letter to his father, using his left hand since his right was still too badly burned for penmanship:

> I had never been able to understand why men jumped from a burning plane to their certain death below, but I knew then that death did not seem to matter at all. The only thing in the world that I wanted to do was to get out of that pain, so I jerked off my belt and started to hop out when it flashed through my mind that I was leaving Eddie to burn up while I died easy; so I thought I would take one crack at it instead of doing him a yellow trick. I pulled out of a spin and dived vertically, opening the throttle up wide, and taking the one chance of burning out the gas in the motor, though I did not believe there was any chance at all; but to my surprise the fire did go out. Meanwhile I had fallen partially on my back, and had an awful job keeping from falling from the plane, because I had no belt.

Cooper had made a three-point landing in a field far behind German lines by controlling the stick between his knees, his hands and face seared by the fire in his engine. Edward C. Leonard, his observer, opened his eyes and smiled. He had been shot through the neck, fainted from loss of blood, and then regained consciousness. Immediately a German victor flew over the field at fifty feet, hand-signaling for the Americans to step away from their airplane. He turned and came back, landing beside the two Yanks, Leonard lying on the ground, Cooper now almost helpless in fiery agony. The German, an ace wearing an Iron Cross of the First Class, saluted, extended his hand for their pistols, and claimed them prisoner. German garrison troops were running across the field, and the ace, who did not reveal his name, had field medics attending them at once.

The following afternoon Cooper, who faced only a short time as a prisoner of war, was interrogated by a German Intelligence officer. How many troops did the Americans have in training at home? Cooper knew there were around two million, so he promptly said twenty-five million. The German gave up on Cooper's obvious falsehood and began confiding in him that Germany could no longer hope to win the war, but could win a good peace.

The airmen of World War I were a wild, irrepressible bunch, their escapades justly legendary, and Americans were no exception. When American soldiers went on leave, it was the airmen who most likely could be seen drinking champagne out of a woman's slipper, or dancing barefoot on a table to an accompaniment of soup-plates used as cymbals. Some were known to have cut the chains anchoring captured field guns to the Arc de Triomphe and raced the guns down the Champs Élysées. Once in a restaurant a group of aviators stuffed hard rolls with cherry jam and bounced them off the ears of unwary staff majors. In many places these aviators were banned from the premises—a crystal chandelier could stand just so many skin-the-cats.

They were like wild fraternity brothers, with a grim humor impossible to suppress on a flying field, on leave, or in a hospital. There was one flyer who escaped from a ward at Angers in bandages, drainage tubes, and pajamas, and hired two French youths to push him to a café in a hand cart. He returned at two A.M. as drunk as a lord and twice as happy, pish-tushing an infuriated surgeon, bussing the cheek of a head nurse with a famous temper. He bore presents for everyone in the ward; one of the wounded, in heavy plaster, his legs suspended by pulleys, received a tennis racket and a child's jump-rope with painted wooden handles.

Compared to the infantryman, the airman lived in splendor, with a roof over his head, clean sheets, good food and drink—all the comforts of home. But no Doughboy on the ground below ever begrudged the flyers their heralded fame; he envied them and admired them.

13

Capturing the Saint-Quentin Tunnel

As FOCH had demonstrated to T. Bentley Mott with his flurry of lefts and rights, the entire Allied line was now pressing the offensive, though not everywhere on the long front could the attacks be coordinated on the same day and hour. To the left of the Meuse-Argonne sector the French armies were pressing forward, and further west the British also were smashing at German defenses. One of the biggest obstacles on the British front was the Saint-Quentin Tunnel complex. In order to help them crack it the British asked for, and Pershing gave them, two of his most promising outfits, the U.S. 27th and 30th Divisions, which had been training in the British sector for several months.

The Saint-Quentin Tunnel was an important link in a canal system connecting the Scheldt and Somme rivers, built in the 19th century. The tunnel through which the canal ran was about three miles long, and was impregnable to artillery fire. The Germans had made it an important bastion in their Hindenburg Line, which stretched over a hundred miles behind the front. They had filled the tunnel with enough barges to house an entire German division and had protected the tunnel mouth at each end with a three-deep trench system, each trench faced with belts of barbed wire fantastically woven about concrete pillboxes that had been placed on every mound of high ground. Extra passageways had been dug from the tunnel into bombproofs beneath the three trench lines, hideouts so deep that thirty wooden steps led down to them. It was an underground city, with electric lights and telephone systems. The steep canal cut outside each entrance to the tunnel was festooned with shacks and shanties resembling a hobo jugle, but dug into the shambles were concrete cubicles with steel casemates baring the fangs of machine guns.

The U.S. 27th Division was made up of lads from all over New York State, farmers and woodsmen sharing billets with slum-bred and blue-blooded boys from the five boroughs of America's biggest city. Only the "Fighting Sixty-ninth" was missing, having been assigned to the 42nd Rainbow Division as the 165th U.S. Infantry Regiment. The 27th's major general was John F. O'Ryan, a lawyer who had taken up soldiering on a fulltime basis as commander of his state's National Guard. His men wore the constellation of Orion as a shoulder patch in honor of his name. The 30th Division was made up of National Guard troops from South Carolina, North Carolina, and Tennessee. Since Andrew Jackson had been born in the first state, mixed his law studies with cockfighting, drinking, and gambling in the second, and made his home in the third, they called themselves "The Old Hickory Division." Their major general was Edward M. Lewis, who before his promotion had commanded the Doughboy brigade of the 2nd Division at Vaux.

The two divisions had undergone all their training with the British since their arrival in France, so if any American troops were to be chosen to stay with the Tommies it was logical the lads of the 27th and 30th be selected. The British had briefed them with care and thoroughness, but there had been some problems, too. Surprisingly, for many a Doughboy there was a greater language barrier between him and a Tommie than between the Yank and a Frenchman. Americans training with the French had interpreters; they also had the benefit of the Frenchman's Gallic gestures.

In his two-volume history of the 27th Division, written after the war, General O'Ryan set down as an example of the problems the dialog of a British officer who was a wizard in trench mortars speaking to a Yank who was hoping to learn about them:

> I came over as a subaltern in the 6th Don Aac . . . I visited a lot of places of the R.A.M.C., but hardly was I on the way with this work when I got a chit from the G.O.C., R.F.A., of the 40th Don Aac . . . what I was really interested in was the Tock Emmas, with the Emma G's as second choice . . .

It would have required an interpreter to explain to the befuddled Yank that the speaker was an artilleryman who had been assigned to the Royal Army Medical Corps; that the General Officer Commanding, Royal Field Artillery, of the 40th Division's field artillery had wanted him, that his preference was trench mortars, with machine guns next. The British converted the alphabet into words: "Tock" for "T," "Emma" for "M," and so forth. Hence, "Tock Emmas" were trench mortars, and "Emma G's" machine guns.

The contrast between the private language of the Tommie and the expressiveness of the poilu was remarkable. Many a Doughboy platoon leader, relieving a Frenchman on the front line in the dead of night, had a far better idea of what was going on when the Frenchman simply said, "*Les boches* [he pointed] *sont là. Beaucoup mitrailleuses là.*" He uttered a child's "rat-a-a-a-rat" sound of imaginary machine guns, pointing to a high spot to his right. "*Prenez-garde, monsieur! Boom-boom! Terrible! Là!*" He made a sweeping movement with his arm, and then squatted and imitated the short, ugly bark of trench mortars, ending with a "whom" to indicate a gap in the trenches where a wise soldier would not throw his shadow in daylight hours. Having thus

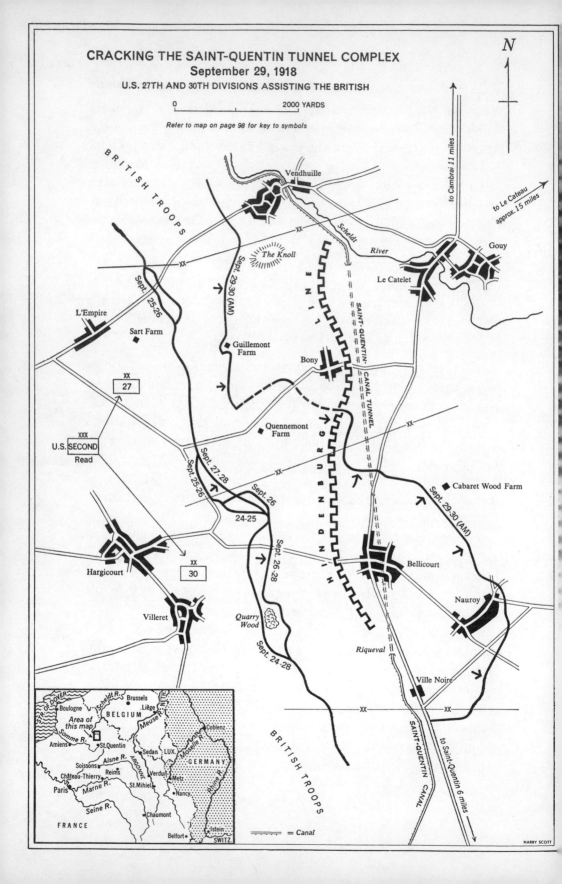

CRACKING THE SAINT-QUENTIN TUNNEL COMPLEX
September 29, 1918
U.S. 27TH AND 30TH DIVISIONS ASSISTING THE BRITISH

0   2000 YARDS

Refer to map on page 98 for key to symbols

N

BRITISH TROOPS

to Cambrai 11 miles

to Le Cateau
approx. 15 miles

Vendhuille

The Knoll

Scheldt

River

Gouy

Le Catelet

Sept. 29-30 (AM)

L'Empire

Sept. 25-26

Sart Farm

Guillemont
Farm

Bony

SAINT-QUENTIN
CANAL TUNNEL

XX
27

Quennemont
Farm

HINDENBURG LINE

Sept. 27-28

Sept. 25-26

U.S. SECOND
Read
XXX

Sept. 26

24-25

Cabaret Wood Farm

Sept. 29-30 (AM)

Hargicourt

XX
30

Sept. 26-28

Bellicourt

Nauroy

Villeret

Quarry
Wood

Riqueval

Ville Noire

Sept. 24-28

BRITISH
TROOPS

SAINT-QUENTIN CANAL

to Saint-Quentin 6 miles

STR. OF DOVER
Boulogne
Scheldt R.
Brussels
Liège
BELGIUM
Area of
this map
NETH.
Meuse R.
Coblenz
Somme R.
Amiens
St.Quentin
Sedan
LUX.
GERMANY
Soissons
Aisne R.
Château-Thierry
Reims
ARGONNE
Verdun
Metz
Moselle R.
Rhine R.
Paris
Marne R.
St.Mihiel
Nancy
Seine R.
Chaumont
Istein
Belfort
SWITZ.
FRANCE

= Canal

HARRY SCOTT

described the situation, he simply said, *"Bon secteur. Au 'voir, m'sieu,"* and hustled back to whatever was awaiting him behind the lines.

The men of the 27th and 30th Divisions eventually learned the Tommie military lingo and fighting techniques, and in September they had been moved eastward from Flanders to the Somme River region. They had become expert with British-made Vickers machine guns, Stokes mortars, and Lewis guns, and they were ready. Sir Douglas Haig, the British Commander in Chief, had decided they were just what he wanted to break the powerful Saint-Quentin Tunnel defenses.

The attack was scheduled for six o'clock in the morning on September 29, with the 27th Division on the left, the 30th in the center, and the British 46th Division on the right. The assault of the U.S. 30th and the British 46th went off like clockwork. Doughboys and Tommies fought through three belts of wire, overran the three trench systems, blocked the southern entrance to the tunnel, and seized the towns of Bellicourt and Nauroy. By nightfall they had captured 47 German officers and 1,434 men. But things went badly from the start for the 27th Division which faced very rough German positions guarding the northern half of the tunnel and had no expert British division on its flank.

First of all, the British division it was to relieve had been unable to secure jump-off lines, so the 27th sent a regiment through the British two days before the attack to try to take the lines. After a day of furious fighting, in which nearly all of the officers were killed or wounded, the Germans were still in possession of the lines except for a few patches held by New Yorkers.

Among these was Second Lieutenant William B. Turner. By the early part of the evening of September 27 he had only nine men left in his section. When a German machine gun discovered them and opened fire, Turner charged the gun alone and pistoled its crew to death. Then he moved on to a second gun in a nearby trench. He had killed one of its gunners when his nine men arrived and finished off the rest. He was now bearing three wounds, but he led his men on to a zigzag in the same trench that concealed more Germans, Turner and his men overcoming them in hand-to-hand combat. Now out of ammunition, Turner seized a German rifle with bayonet and led his men on to a fourth position, capturing it in a furious charge of rifle bullets and bayonets. He had now reached his assigned objective, but like the British the day before, he was not long in possession of it. The enemy came in force at the Yanks, killed Turner and captured the survivors among his men.

Turner's fate was shared by many. On the following day, September 28, the British refused to permit another attack to seize the jump-off lines without a preliminary artillery barrage, and they did not dare shell the area for fear that some New Yorkers were still there. Thus the full 27th Division now faced the prospect, the next day, of beginning a major assault with a severe handicap.

When the creeping barrage began advancing over German lines at 6 A.M. on September 29, the New Yorkers were too far behind to be able to follow it and its temporary protection. Instead they spent thirty minutes in a berserk fight to seize their own jump-off lines, grappling with Germans who reappeared as soon as the barrage passed, some in bullet-proof vests. Only after the jump-off lines were secured were they able to go forward, and now, without the screen of their own artillery, many New York Guardsmen gave up their lives that morning in an area of fifteen hundred square yards.

By sunset the 107th Infantry Regiment of the 27th Division had 227 officers and men killed and 658 wounded. The Australians had come up at noon with orders to plug serious gaps and pass through the stricken regiment. Things really went awry then, for the survivors of the 107th and other American regiments were ordered to hold fast and refused to do so. Doughboy platoons went forward with the Aussies, and attacking lines became a mixture of Aussies and Yanks following the orders of Australian captains. The conduct of the Yanks delighted the men from down under, and side-by-side the soldiers of the two nations set forth to take the last German strongpoints guarding the northern half of the tunnel. It took another twenty-four hours, but the Aussies and Yanks of the 27th Division finally overcame such German bastions as "The Knoll," and pushed forward until they were even with the advance achieved earlier by the U.S. 30th and British 46th Divisions. By the evening of September 30, the capture of the Saint-Quentin Tunnel was accomplished.

The Australian commander, Lieutenant General Sir John Monash, wrote of the free-lances who joined his men, expressing what "great pleasure it has been to me and to the troops of the Australian Army Corps to have been so closely allied to you in the recent very important battle operations which have resulted in the breaking through of the Main Hindenburg Line." "So closely allied" was the phrase the Doughboys liked, though their conduct had been highly irregular and was criticized in later staff studies.

By the end of the war the 30th Division had won more Medals of Honor than any other division. Its valor shone on this day with many illustrious individual performances, as did the 27th's, whose men showed such guts in the face of adversity. One hidden machine gun that surprised the 30th Division's Sergeant Joseph B. Adkinson's second-wave platoon so enraged the sergeant that he charged it in the wide open, miraculously unscathed, and kicked the machine gun into the gunners' faces. The rest of Adkinson's platoon arrived to find three Germans busily turning the gun to face their own men, under the sergeant's directions.

Three other Yanks, Sergeant John C. Latham, and Corporals Alan L. Eggers and Thomas E. O'Shea, fighting in isolation on the summit of the tunnel, came to the rescue of a disabled tank crew. O'Shea stopped a bullet that would prove fatal, but Latham and Eggers pulled out a wounded officer and two wounded sergeants and dragged them to a nearby shell hole. They were under fierce fire and in danger of counterattacks, so one of the tank crew, Sergeant Frank J. Williams, hobbled back to the tank and operated the six-pounder cannon for some time until it was knocked out by an armor-piercing shell. When Williams returned to the shell hole they all agreed they were goners unless they had more firepower. Accordingly, Williams, Eggers, and Latham returned to the tank and dismantled and brought back the Hotchkiss machine gun, which kept their shell hole inviolate until darkness came and they were able to return to their own lines with the wounded and the Hotchkiss gun. Adkinson, Latham, Eggers, and the dying O'Shea were all awarded the Medal of Honor; Williams, the Distinguished Service Cross.

Both U.S. divisions, after resting, continued on with the British into October. They never received the publicity back home that was heaped on their brothers in the Argonne, but they suffered about the same number of casualties: the 30th 7,455 officers and men, the 27th 8,088—the variance in figures attributable to that fatal jump-off line on September 29. The British were very pleased with them, and Pershing would have been delighted to have them both. In fact, after the initial success on September 26, he could have used them almost anywhere on his Meuse-Argonne line.

Chapter

14

Slowdown on the Meuse-Argonne Front

AFTER the first day's assault
in the Meuse-Argonne sector, the initial rush of the American
First Army was slowed to a crawl, and in some places held up altogether. Bullard's III Corps on the right was stopped in its tracks
before the village of Brieulles on the Meuse. In the center, the
crucial hill of Montfaucon fell to the 37th and 79th Divisions of
Cameron's V corps the second day, September 27th, but by this
time it was too late to exploit a breakthrough.

Liggett's I Corps on the left was slowed like the other two corps.
The Pennsylvanians of the 28th Division, in Liggett's center,
fared particularly badly. Two thirds of its troops were in the
open valley of the Aire River, exposed to merciless shelling from
the heights on either side. Over a period of twelve days the Pennsylvanians measured their gains in inches, and their ranks were
decimated by 6,149 casualties.

The 77th Division on Liggett's left pushed forward in the
depths of the Argonne Forest, taking one fortified pavilion after
another, harassed by German rear guards. These Argonne pavil-

ions were not only fortresses; some were paradise camps for prime German divisions that had earned rest and recreation. The 77th looted the Bagatelle Pavilion on the second day of the offensive. Its scout platoons were almost unable to believe that the Aladdin-like caves, tastefully decorated blockhouses, and chalets were real. They were stocked with books, the best of liquors, and cigars, the surrounding grounds beautifully landscaped. The Doughboys made off with everything they could carry, but their pockets were not capable of holding a tenth of the bottles they wanted.

The Yanks soon became wary of the tricks used by the Germans around these pavilions. On September 28 an American scout platoon captured outpost trenches of the Saint Hubert Pavilion and accepted the surrender of German troops crying *"Kamerad"* with hands held skyward. The Doughboys had their rifles lowered as the two groups approached each other when suddenly a German assault team broke through the bushes and cut the American platoon to pieces as the surrendering decoys dived for cover. But the enemy had not reckoned on Lieutenant Dwight H. Schaffner, who, just coming up, stood upon a parapet with a Chauchat and cut down the attackers. He then charged with his pistol, wounding the German captain who had ordered the ruse, dragging him back unaided and forcing that treacherous officer to divulge the disposition of forces ahead. Schaffner now knew more about the Germans than they knew about the Yanks, a rare circumstance in that forest. Schaffner was awarded the Medal of Honor, his performance having been witnessed by wounded Doughboys littering the ground.

By September 30 the green 35th Division on the right of Liggett's I Corps (see map, page 104) was on its way to becoming a first-class fighting outfit. That afternoon, one of the American balloonists whom Rickenbacker and his fellow pilots were defending against German aviators was shot up by a Fokker. But just before he went down he telephoned a report to the 110th Field Signal Battalion that an unwary Doughboy infantry battalion crouching at the base of a slope was about to be attacked on its left flank by a strong German unit. Telephone wires having been cut by enemy fire, the strongest runner of the Signal Battalion was selected to get this information to a battery of the 35th's artillery up ahead. If he could get there in time there was a chance the battery could break up the German attack with a well-aimed barrage.

Runners are often among those neglected in regimental histories. They were chosen for strength, agility, and persistence. The 110th Field Signal Battalion chose Paul Shaffer to make the run that afternoon through the shell-roaring death. Shaffer's own tale reveals something of the quality and temper of himself and his buddies in the green 35th Division, a future United States president among them.

When I was twenty, I got the White House greetings. I put my occupation down as a blacksmith and was attached to the Signal Corps, though I didn't know a dot from a dash, and had never seen a wireless set. It turned out that a field signal battalion was allowed three pack horses to carry wireless batteries and I was to go along to shoe them. I had a curious dingus on my sleeve, and my pay was something between corporal and sergeant. My buddies said I was a corporal sergeant.

We reached Le Havre on a British ship in April, 1918, and were sent to Flanders to learn trench-warfare signals from the British. General Pershing came down to inspect us, and took my horses for his artillery. I just carried a one-horse load of storage batteries on my back into the Flanders mud three times.

My job in reserve was mostly lifting heavy things when I wasn't running messages. I knew I ought to tell the major to send me back to a remount depot where I could do a lot of good. But, hell, when you get around buddies that have to have messages when enemy fire has torn up your wires, you can't tear yourself away. After Saint-Mihiel, we had trucks for the batteries, and I walked about a hundred miles in five nights in a seventy-two-pound pack as light as a feather, except my clothes were always dripping wet as I stood under trees during the day . . . and when they gave me the message that afternoon [September 30], it was for the Truman battery.

I set out on the run, jumping into shell holes when I heard one with my name on it, or crashing myself against outcroppings when those big ones shrieked, "Where are you, Corporal Sergeant Shaffer?" I doubt any blacksmith ever ran so fast. I reached the battery in nothing flat, as muddy as an alligator, all the skin off my nose. Captain Harry S. Truman was standing there, his tin hat pushed on the back of his head, directing salvos into some spot toward the northeast. He was a banty officer in spectacles, and when he read my message he started runnin' and cussin' all at the same time, shouting for the guns to turn northwest. He ran about a hundred yards to a little knoll, and what he saw didn't need binoculars. I never heard a man cuss so well or so intelligently, and I'd shoed a million mules. He was shouting back ranges and giving bearings.

The battery didn't say a word. They must have figured the cap'n could do the cussin' for the whole outfit. It was a great sight, like the center ring in Barnum and Bailey at the close of the show, everything clockwork, setting fuses, cutting fuses, slapping shells into breeches and jerking lanyards before the man hardly had time to bolt the door. Shell casings were flipping back like a juggler's act, clanging on tin hats of the ammunition passers, the guns just spitting fire—spit-spit-spit-spit.

Then Captain Truman ran down the knoll and cussed 'em to fire even faster. When he ran back up the hill still cussin', I forgot how I didn't want to get killed and I ran with him. I couldn't see our infantry. It must have been driven back to the little knoll, trying to crawl around and change front. Beyond it was some mighty fine grazing land, and at the far end a clump of woods, pretty leaves still on the autumn trees. The leaves were falling fast, shells breaking into them. This time Captain Truman had his binoculars on them. I finally made out what he saw. There were groups of Germans at the edge of the woods, stooping low and coming on slowly with machine guns on their hips, held by shoulder straps. He shouted some cusswords filled with figures down to the battery, and shells started breaking into the enemy clumps. Whole legs were soon flying through the air. He really broke up that counterattack. He was still there being shot at when I came to my senses and got off the knoll.

I never saw the cussin' captain again until I voted for him in

1948. That night the First Division relieved us. "What's the trouble around here?" some of their guys said. "Anything need fixin'?" It sure was time.

In five days of some of the fiercest fighting of the war, Corporal Sergeant Shaffer, Captain Harry S. Truman, and their buddies in the 35th Division had managed to advance six miles to the right of the Aire River at tremendous cost. Relieved by the veterans and replacements of the Big Red One on October 1, the survivors of the 35th went back to lick their wounds, delouse, and mourn their losses. Scheduled to fight again November 14, the war ended before they had a chance to show their mettle a second time.

Chapter

15

The Lost Battalion

O<small>N THE NIGHT</small> of October 1 Hunter Liggett ordered the 77th Division on the extreme left flank of his I Corps to attack the Palette Pavilion deep in the Argonne Forest at 6:30 A.M. the next day. This pavilion was the toughest position the 77th had yet faced, its heights protected by cliffs, woods, and undergrowth, and with shallow trenches defending its southern slopes. The position was much prized by the enemy, for it commanded not only the dense southern forests of the Argonne, but a spur valley from the Aisne River where the French troops flanking the New Yorkers were trying to advance.

The 77th Division's commander, Major General Robert Alexander, selected the 1st and 2nd Battalions of the 308th Infantry Regiment for the attack. Major Charles W. Whittlesey commanded the 1st Battalion, which would lead the assault; Captain George G. McMurtry commanded the 2nd Battalion and would support Whittlesey. Because of losses in the preceding six days, instead of sixteen hundred men Whittlesey and McMurtry had between them a little less than half that number.

After a barrage from a regiment of supporting field artillery Whittlesey plunged forward at 6:30 A.M., McMurtry following, two machine-gun companies going along. They did not attack alone, for the entire I Corps front went forward at the same time, and everywhere the attack failed in a shocking repulse, with stretcher-bearers and groaning wounded everywhere. But Pershing's orders were for each division in each corps to press forward looking after its own flanks, and so General Alexander ordered the 77th to resume its attack at 1:30 in the afternoon. This gave Whittlesey and McMurtry time to regroup their men and let them chew on field rations before the next assault. Then, promptly at 1:30 P.M., the division attacked again and Whittlesey broke through, McMurtry following, crossing wide bands of rusty barbed wire, overruning German trenches, killing enemy flankers with Hotchkiss heavy tripod machine guns. Storming on, they crossed a fearsome ravine that sliced across their front and pressed forward until they reached a smaller ravine just south of their objective for the day, the Charlevaux Mill. On the north side of this ravine they found a road that ran along the side of a hill. Whittlesey dug in along this road to await the inevitable German counterattack, setting up his machine gunners on his flanks. The Germans were above him, but the hill was so steep that German gunners could not bring their guns to bear on the Yanks.

Whittlesey and McMurtry had set out with about 675 men, and they had lost 90 in the advance. The number of enemy casualties was unknown; the Yanks had taken two officers and twenty-eight men prisoner and captured two machine guns. Most of the German defenders had fallen back to stronger positions, taking their guns with them and leaving a mile of trenches unmanned. But Whittlesey and McMurtry were in good shape, with a line of runner posts extending back to Brigade headquarters. It was now up to the rest of the 77th Division and the French troops on the left to come up even with Whittlesey's advance so that the French and reinforced Doughboys could take the Charlevaux Mill position.

As the afternoon of October 2 waned, General Alexander ordered the 307th Infantry Regiment to join Whittlesey. The 307th promptly attacked, but the supporting troops, with the exception of one company, never reached the trapped battalion. Morning of October 3 found the majority of the 307th, having lost their way, dazedly facing the French flank in the Aisne valley. Only Captain Nelson K. Holderman, with the eyes of a lynx and the heart of a leopard, had been able to lead the ninety-seven survivors of K Company, 307th Infantry Regiment, up to Whittlesey's position that morning.

In the meantime, Whittlesey had dispatched Lieutenant Wilhelm with a small force to backtrail in hopes of bringing up some of his missing men and any reinforcements that might have become lost. Wilhelm never made it, for early that morning the Germans had reoccupied the mile of empty trenches with machine gunners, mortar men, and infantry, capturing or driving off Whittlesey's runner posts. Wilhelm was surrounded but ordered Lieutenant Lenke back to Whittlesey's command while he covered for him. Lenke made it with nineteen men. Wilhelm eventually reached the division's main line with a few survivors.

When Lenke got back, Whittlesey knew that he was bagged: 650 Doughboys (elements of three infantry battalions plus his machine gunners) were trapped in a slender oval 70 yards deep and 350 yards long by a fresh German division of riflemen, machine gunners, flame throwers, and mortarmen skillfully positioned around them at a distance of about two hundred yards. At this point, Whittlesey sent two of his eight carrier pigeons to Alexander, asking for ammunition, rations, and support, and giving his approximate whereabouts.

At dawn that same morning, October 3, General Alexander made his second move to rescue Whittlesey's group, attacking with both brigades and gaining nothing. One of the company commanders described it:

> The heavy fog had kept the powder smoke down and as morning dawned I found myself with two runners adrift in a blind world of whiteness and noise, groping over something like the surface of the moon. One literally could not see two yards and everywhere the ground rose into bare pinnacles and ridges or descended into bottomless chasms, half-filled with rusty tangles

of wire. . . . At the end of two hours I had collected two squads of infantry with a few engineers and so, with forces joined, we pushed on into the thickest jungle I have ever seen and it seemed to go on forever. And by one o'clock, in a fifteen-foot trench with unscalable walls of mud and a stream along its bottom, I knew where nothing was except the guide, my Company Headquarters and half a platoon.

Another attempt to reach Whittlesey was made around four o'clock that afternoon, October 3, one battalion losing five officers and two hundred men before it was stopped cold. The Germans were furious that inexperienced Doughboys had progressed for six days into what the German Staff considered impregnable positions. The Germans had designed a defense in depth of heavy machine guns, each gun positioned to fire on its neighbor so that if one gun was captured the captors could be cut down by a flanking gun. Nothing but an attack of tanks could overrun these nests, and the few tanks available in 1918 were useless in ravine terrain.

At 5:30 A.M. the next day, October 4, still another attempt was made to break through to Whittlesey. This time Brigadier General Evan M. Johnson tried to lead his brigade of the 77th Division through the hole Whittlesey had torn in German wire two days before. As had happened every other time, Johnson met fierce resistance and was unable to make any sizable gains against the tenacious Germans.

By the following day, October 5, Whittlesey was beginning to suffer severely. He had been trapped on his road three nights now. He had no food and little water. His medical supplies were exhausted, about half his men wounded, many d.... McMurtry was hobbling about on a tree-branch crutch w.... knee the size of a football, where shrapnel fragments we.... ring. Holderman, using a rifle for a crutch, had three w.... thus far, one of them a piece of the wooden stick from a potato-masher grenade lodged in his back. The Germans tormented them with an avalanche of grenades hurled on signal from the hill above, the shouts of the German sergeants counting off *ein, zwei, drei* (one, two, three) clearly audible to the Yanks. The survivors were dug in everywhere, too feeble to bury their own dead. Field medics crawled to cadavers and stripped off blood-soaked bandages to use them again on freshly wounded men, while other wounded rifled the pockets of the dead in hopes of finding a morsel of chocolate, a few shreds of tobacco. When a few French and American shells accidentially landed among them, Whittlesey sent more of his pigeons, urgently asking all artillery counterfire to cease.

Many attempts were made by aviators of the 50th Aero Squadron to locate Whittlesey's group and drop them food and ammunition. They flew "Flaming Coffins" just over treetop level in the hopes of spotting, through the autumn haze and smoke, the small white markers set out by the trapped Yanks as guidance for the pilots. On the morning of October 5 Lieutenants Harold Goettler and Erwin Bleckley, pilot and observer, made several passes at two hundred feet over the ravine, dropping medical supplies and food as best they could while German machine gunners shot their plane's fabric into sievelike patterns. Miraculously they got away and made it back to their field. That afternoon they returned for another attempt. As they swooped in at treetop level, German machine-gun and rifle fire from the hill above mortally wounded both men, but Goettler lived long enough to pull back on his stick and land his plane in French front lines on the left flank of the 77th Division. Both Goettler and Bleckley were awarded the Medal of Honor, posthumously.

Also on October 5, the French pushed up the Aisne valley to the left of the Americans in a fine advance, and for a few minutes they captured and held the Palette Pavilion beyond the Charlevaux Mill. But Whittlesey, trapped one thousand yards below the Charlevaux Mill, was unable to do anything to help the French, who were driven out by counterattacks.

It was the same story on October 6. Liggett ordered another attack along his I Corps front, and no man could hear his own voice in the deafening noise that roared through the valley of the Aire and the Argonne Forest that morning; yet lines were unchanged around Whittlesey when it was over. The French then asked permission to renew shelling of the Mill positions, but Brigadier General Johnson was quick to protest that Whittlesey was still there. All of the Yanks assumed, and never once doubted, that Whittlesey would never surrender.

There was one ray of hope on October 6 to those trying to rescue the trapped Doughboys. A lieutenant and two privates from Whittlesey's group arrived back at the main division line, having managed to filter through the surrounding Germans. They had left Whittlesey on October 5 at dusk, had spent three stealthy hours during the night in the midst of sleeping Germans in an enemy bivouac, and had then shot their way out. They were taken to Lieutenant Colonel Eugene H. Houghton, commander of the 307th Infantry Regiment, who had had three years of experience with the Canadian army before 1918. Houghton went to General Alexander and told him that on the basis of the information supplied by these three men he, Houghton, believed he could get his regiment to Whittlesey through a gap in German wire. Alexander decided the attempt would be made the next day, along with a general attack.

At daybreak, October 7, a private in McMurtry's H Company, with eight buddies, disobeyed orders and left the positions on the road and slipped through the forest hoping to retrieve a package of rations that aviators had dropped nearby. The nine famished lads were ambushed by a German patrol. Five were killed, the other four wounded and taken prisoner. One of their German captors was Lieutenant Fritz Printz, a platoon commander in the 67th Reserve Division who had spent six years in Spokane, Washington, before the war. Printz suggested to his major that a plea to surrender sent back to Whittlesey by one of the wounded Doughboy prisoners might succeed in ending the stubborn and embarrassing American resistance, and prevent further bloodshed. The major agreed to try it.

Accordingly, Private Lowell R. Hollingshead, the insubordinate but honorable boy from H Company, was selected to carry the plea back to Whittlesey. The prisoner refused, and then was entreated to do so in the name of humanity. Hollingshead agreed on condition that the note clear his name with his commanding officer. The note was written, the prisoner blindfolded and released near the machine-gun flank of the road. He made his way through American lines and handed the note to Whittlesey at four o'clock in the afternoon of October 7. It read:

To the Commanding Officer—Infantry, 77th American Division

SIR: The bearer of this present, Private Hollingshead, has been taken prisoner by us. He refused to give the German Intelligence Officer any answer to his questions, and is quite an honorable fellow, doing honor to his Fatherland in the strictest sense of the word.

He has been charged against his will, believing that he is doing wrong to his country to carry forward this present letter to the officer in charge of the battalion of the 77th Division, with the purpose to recommend this commander to surrender with his forces, as it would be quite useless to resist anymore, in view of present conditions.

The suffering of your wounded men can be heard over here in the German lines, and we are appealing to your humane sentiments to stop. A white flag shown by one of your men will tell us that you agree with these conditions. Please treat Private Hollingshead as an honorable man. He is quite a soldier. We envy you.   THE GERMAN COMMANDING OFFICER

Whittlesey sent no reply to the note, but grapevine carried news of it along the foxholes of the road, and a chorus began when a wounded man rose on one elbow and shouted down the valley, "Come and get us!" It was the German commander's first news of the unknown Doughboy commander's reaction, but scores of other Yanks soon joined in. The German commander's sentiments now changed. He ordered his men to attack with flame throwers on the right flank where there was the one remaining Hotchkiss gunner. As the German *Flamenwerfer* men charged, their deadly weapon spouting liquid fire, the Hotchkiss gunner fired at them pointblank, igniting their fuel tank and kindling the entire German assault team into human torches.

Many years afterward, Walter Baldwin, who was a corporal on the road that day, could recall the figure of his captain, Holderman, standing erect by using a pair of rifles as crutches, giving the gunner, Sergeant George Hauck, fire cover with his Colt .45. The captain, suffering from four previous wounds, the stick of a potato-masher grenade still in his back, got his fifth wound about the time he got his fifth German.

On the main line of the 77th, the general attack had gone off as scheduled on the morning of October 7. This time the information that Lieutenant Colonel Houghton had gained paid off. Patrols got through the gap in the wire he had discovered, and the 307th Infantry Regiment poured in to turn the German flank. Brigadier General Johnson, an old Apache fighter, attacked in the first wave as if he were a private soldier. The division's whole front swarmed through behind Johnson and Houghton.

The machine gunner on Whittlesey's road, with Holderman giving pistol support, was still firing sporadic bursts when, far away, Doughboys heard the familiar chatter of Hotchkiss guns, the curious, racking coughs of the Chauchats, and soon, nearby, the Springfield's high-pitched whine. Presently a new Doughboy arrived, one never seen before. He was carrying on his bayonet a sack with a few cans of corned beef. Then many others appeared, flooding the ravine, pushing up to the road and above, killing Germans and driving the rest off the fatal hill. "Look at 'em run, the Heinie bastards!" shouted the wounded as a new officer went the rounds of festering men with a mess-kit spoon, offering every man a taste of his first food in five days.

Many of the wounded were too weak to walk; some had cramps from eating the bark of trees. The survivors told of the avalanches of potato-masher grenades and motar shells from above; of flank attacks, frontal assaults, ruses; of a Yank aviator who succeeded in directing a bombardment of the hill above by hovering over it and signaling, "*Fire on me*"; of their shouts of joy when German corpses were blown sky-high as artillery found the range.

Many of them wanted to know the fate of their eighth, and last, carrier pigeon, *Cher Ami* (Dear Friend). The little bird had been released that morning, after American shells again fell among them, but he had perched in a treetop with the message wrapped around his leg, not wishing to brave the shrapnel coursing through the skies. He was sent on his way when the pigeon man, Omer Richards, climbed the tree under fire and scolded him.

Richards and the others were assured that *Cher Ami* was back at the pigeon wagon, minus an eye and a leg, the division veterinary surgeon in attendance, and that he would recover. The men back there were carving a wooden leg or two for *Cher Ami*, who was going to be retired and, someday, be mounted in a glass case at the Smithsonian Institution.

Major Kenney's battalion of the 307th Infantry Regiment was the first to reach Whittlesey with rations and ammunition. Though the sun had set there was still an afterglow on the hills of torture above the road, but it was decided not to attempt an evacuation in the dark. Major General Alexander reached the position on foot at next daybreak, October 8, striding along the road swinging his malacca walking stick, a captured German cigar stuck in his big Scots face. He found a gaunt Whittlesey distributing rations to his wounded; on the road stood 195 unwounded, the remnant of the unconquerable 650 who had won it six days before.

Alexander did not stay long, and he did not say much. He recalled after the war that a sentence from Lord Napier's *History of the Peninsular War* ran through his memory, a description of a battle's aftermath: "The enemy rolled backward down the slope, the rain followed in torrents stained with blood and fifteen hundred unwounded men, the remnant of six thousand unconquerable . . . soldiers, stood triumphant on the fatal hill." As soon as Whittlesey's survivors were ready they marched out to the collecting station with their wounded, McMurtry still on his crutch, the last man to leave the road.

The story of "The Lost Battalion" immediately became a saga rivaling that of the Texas Alamo. It made headlines all over America. Yet actually "The Lost Battalion" was not a battalion, nor was it ever lost. No commander ever knew his whereabouts better than Whittlesey, senior among officers from seven companies of three infantry battalions and the machine-gun elements of a fourth. He had been cut off short of his objective for the day, October 2, with a French division on his left and his own brigade failing to keep pace. He had sent his position back by carrier pigeon, and he had not been out of line by more than ten feet.

Alexander, with Liggett's permission, at once made Major Whittlesey a lieutenant colonel, McMurtry a major, and awarded both of them and Captain Holderman the Medal of Honor. What was left of Whittlesey's command immediately volunteered to remain in the line. The Argonne was their forest now, and the New Yorkers intended to keep advancing until they captured all of it.

Chapter

16

Blanc Mont

WHILE THE 77th Division, deep in the Argonne Forest, was struggling to rescue Major Whittlesey and his "Lost Battalion," the French, holding down a long stretch of front to the left of the American First Army's twenty-five mile sector, were driving north as hard as they could. Just to the left of the U.S. 77th Division was General Henri Gouraud's French Fourth Army. On September 26, the opening day of the Meuse-Argonne offensive, Gouraud's sector ran from the left flank of the 77th Division in the Argonne to the city of Reims, a distance of approximately forty miles, and about midway on this line were some imposing heights on the French landscape called Blanc Mont Ridge (see map, page 148).

What the Saint-Quentin Tunnel represented to Sir Douglas Haig, the British supreme commander, Blanc Mont ("White Mountain") meant to General Gouraud. It, too, was a seemingly invincible bastion that had to be taken. The French attacked Blanc Mont on September 26 and got nowhere against its extremely steep terrain and difficult German defenses. They tried again during the next few days, with the same lack of success. Gouraud knew that if he could capture the heights and bring his artillery batteries of 155s to the summit he could dominate the countryside and force the enemy battle lines to withdraw north to the Aisne.

The old French battle-ax had one empty, flapping sleeve, and his wooden leg was as gnarled as a blackthorn cane. As he stared at the heights, he could think only of how much he needed a brawny American division for such a challenging obstacle. All the veteran Doughboy divisions except the 2nd, with its twin racehorse brigades of Doughboys and Marines, were in the Meuse-Argonne front line or moving up by the end of September, Gouraud learned, so he asked General Pétain to use his influence with Foch to get him the 2nd Division. Foch passed on the request to Pershing and pointed out that the 2nd would actually be in support of Liggett's I Corps on the American First Army's left flank. Pershing agreed to the request and gave the 2nd to Gouraud, though it was one of his four best and most experienced divisions and he sorely needed it. So that it might have Yank reserves, Pershing sent the infantry of the green 36th Lone Star Division of Texas and Oklahoma National Guard to back it up.

The 2nd Division arrived to relieve the stalled French the night of October 1–2. Because of the hasty decision to send them there—a familiar experience for the men of the 2nd ever since they were rushed up to the Château-Thierry gap in June—there was little time for them to study the terrain. But after a brief examination their commander, Major General Lejeune, believed the left face of Blanc Mont's summit would present the roughest problem. Lejeune, a Marine (a well known Marine training base in North Carolina was later named after him), did not want to be accused of favoritism, so he assigned the left face to the Marine brigade, the high mound on the right face to the Doughboys. As it turned out, neither side was easy.

The Germans occupied a position which, when viewed from the air, resembled a starfish with cockleburs atop each of its tentacles, each cocklebur a concrete pillbox. Lejeune wisely decided to leave the center alone and assault each flank, and he expected Doughboys and Marines to meet at the top while the French

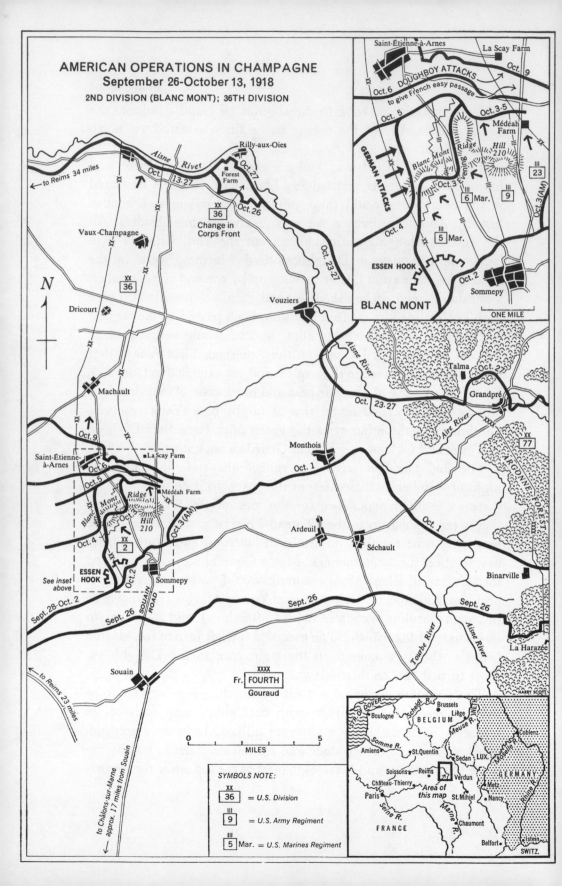

AMERICAN OPERATIONS IN CHAMPAGNE
September 26-October 13, 1918
2ND DIVISION (BLANC MONT); 36TH DIVISION

BLANC MONT (inset, upper right)

Saint-Étienne-à-Arnes
La Scay Farm
Oct. 9
DOUGHBOY ATTACKS
to give French easy passage
Oct. 6
Oct. 5
Médéah Farm
Oct. 3-5
Hill 210
Blanc Mont Ridge
Evans Creek
23
GERMAN ATTACKS
Oct. 3
6 Mar.
9
III (AM) Oct. 3
Oct. 4
5 Mar.
ESSEN HOOK
Oct. 2
Sommepy
ONE MILE

Rilly-aux-Oies
Aisne River
Oct. 13.27
to Reims 34 miles
Forest Farm
Oct. 27
Oct. 26
36
Change in Corps Front
Vaux-Champagne
Oct. 23-27
N
36
Vouziers
Aisne River
Oct. 23-27
Talma
Oct. 27
Dricourt
Grandpré
Aire River
77
Machault
Oct. 9
Monthois
Oct. 1
Saint-Étienne-à-Arnes
Oct. 6
La Scay Farm
Oct. 5
Médéah Farm
Ridge
Oct. 3
Blanc Mont
Hill 210
Oct. 3 (AM)
Ardeuil
Oct. 1
Oct. 4
2
Séchault
ESSEN HOOK
See inset above
Oct. 2
Binarville
Sommepy
SOUAIN ROAD
Sept. 28-Oct. 2
Sept. 26
Sept. 26
Sept. 26
Tourbe River
Aisne River
La Harazée
HARRY SCOTT
to Reims 23 miles
Souain
Fr. FOURTH
Gouraud

0 MILES 5

SYMBOLS NOTE:

36 = U.S. Division

9 = U.S. Army Regiment

5 Mar. = U.S. Marines Regiment

to Châlons-sur-Marne approx. 17 miles from Souain

STR. OF DOVER
Boulogne
Brussels
Liège
BELGIUM
Scheldt R.
Meuse R.
RHINE R.
Coblenz
Somme R.
Amiens
St.Quentin
Sedan
LUX.
Moselle R.
Soissons
Reims
Verdun
Metz
GERMANY
Rhine R.
Paris
Château-Thierry
Marne R.
St. Mihiel
Nancy
Area of this map
Seine R.
Chaumont
FRANCE
Belfort
Istein
SWITZ.

kept pace on each side over lower and easier ground. It was a good plan so long as the French kept up.

On the morning of October 2 the Marine brigade on the left noisily jumped the gun and took the German advanced line, mopping up grenadiers and machine gunners with the customary shouts and cries. They were now in a suitable jumping-off place, ready to follow the next morning's barrage. On the far right, the Doughboy brigade was assured by the French that the poilus already held a suitable jump-off line for the next day's attack, and when the barrage opened the next morning the Yanks could pass through them on their way forward. Unfortunately, during the night of October 2–3 the Germans drove out the French front line, and Doughboy brigade commander Hanson E. Ely was not notified.

At dawn of October 3, the 75s and 155s of the division's artillery laid down a perfect barrage, following a deafening four-hour saturation bombardment by heavy French Corps Artillery, and the Yanks went forward to seize the ridge that had stalled Gouraud for seven frustrating days. The Marines got there first, reaching the crest of Blanc Mont knoll in three hours, fighting their way over three miles of naked slopes and treacherous gullies assisted by a battalion of tanks. The French on their left tried to keep up, but were held up by a rocky amphitheater called Essen Hook before they had gone two hundred yards. So the Marines seized the Hook and presented it to the French, who were promptly driven out by a German counterattack, leaving the Marine flank naked once again. No German captain had to have this opportunity pointed out to him, and for the rest of the day German troops poured withering fire into the Marines' exposed left flank, working savagely to regain the lost crest and forcing the Leathernecks to wheel two battalions ninety degrees to the left to stave off enemy assaults. Yet when night fell the Yanks still held the ridge.

On the far right, Hanson Ely's Doughboy brigade stormed ahead on schedule, overran the Germans who had captured the jump-off lines, and raced to follow their barrage. By noon, in spite of slow movement by the French on their right, the Doughboys were a little farther advanced than the Marines, the latter now beleaguered on Essen Hook. Around three o'clock in the afternoon Ely's Doughboy brigade attacked again and penetrated even farther. The gains of both brigades had cost heavily. Colonels like Logan Feland of the Marines and Paul Malone of the Doughboys agreed that October 3, 1918, was the bloodiest day of the war for the bloodiest division in the A.E.F.

The next morning, October 4, the Marines drove north again, and by noon they had come up with Ely's line far across the ridge. That afternoon Doughboys and Marines pushed ahead and won some ground, then lost much of it to German counterattacks. But by nightfall they had succeeded in driving all enemy troops off Blanc Mont.

The loss of Blanc Mont to the Yanks was a crushing blow to the Germans. General Paul von Hindenburg, their supreme commander, knew he would never recover this vital position, and he gave his troops orders to fall back to the Aisne River and make a stand before it. On October 5 Lejeune halted the 2nd Division while the French, now lightly opposed, pushed up on each flank to the 2nd's line. On October 6 both Yanks and poilus slammed into the Germans, the French soldiers revitalized by witnessing the feats of the Americans against supposedly impregnable positions. That night the 71st Infantry Brigade of the 36th Lone Star Division arrived to take over the center, and on October 8 the 2nd Division drove forward with the newcomers to show them how such things were done.

On the night of October 10 the 2nd Division was relieved, the 36th taking over. The 2nd's racehorse brigades of Doughboys and Marines had broken through five miles of Hindenburg's strongest position in the center of the French armies, had taken about two thousand prisoners, killed or wounded countless numbers of the enemy, and suffered casualties of 6,300 officers and men.

The days had been distinguished by innumerable acts of gallantry. Among many others, the Marines mourned the death of a celebrated character. He had entered Belleau Wood in June a warrant gunner already wearing the Medal of Honor ribbon and had earned a Navy Cross there, the Navy's highest award. After Soissons in July, General Harbord named him for a D.S.C. and a promotion. When he learned that Pershing had come down to the Marne to decorate men from the 1st and 2nd Divisions, he swam the river to stand dripping wet before Pershing to receive the cross. He was killed while reorganizing a company to meet one of the counterattacks on Blanc Mont's flank. He was Lieutenant Henry L. Hurlbutt of the 5th Marine Regiment, Medal of Honor, Navy Cross, Distinguished Service Cross, Croix de Guerre with palm.

The Doughboy brigade had its heroes, too. One was a little runner named Frank T. Bart, who was supposed to carry a message back to headquarters to say that his company was held up by machine gunners. Instead, he picked up a Chauchat and ran ahead of the stalled line and killed the German gunners. Frank's short legs had grown tired of carrying messages. Later he duplicated his exploit, and Lejeune asked Pershing to give this lively boy the Medal of Honor.

Back at Pétain's Group of Armies Headquarters, a résumé of the Blanc Mont operation mentioned that, "In the course of the first day's advance, the 5th Regiment of Marines sent a detachment to the [French] IX Corps to help it clean out the German trenches." Inasmuch as the French were two miles from those German trenches at the time, Marine wits devised a new series of verses for the immortal "Mademoiselle from Armentières," one of which ran like this:

> Oh, the general got the Croix de Guerre,
>   Parley-voo.
> Oh, the general got the Croix de Guerre,
>   Parley-voo.
> Yes, the general got the Croix de Guerre,
> But the sonofagun wasn't even there;
>   Hinky-dinky, parley-voo.

The Story of the Doughboys

Hanson E. Ely, who could sometimes laugh when he was not bellowing orders, had his greatest laugh of the war on the day he and Brigadier General Neville of the Marine brigade were holding a council in a captured pillbox. The day was warm, and Neville hung his green Marine overcoat, with its Marine brigadier's insignia on the sleeves, on a nail outside the door. A Doughboy mule skinner, driving by, and unfamiliar with the difference between Army and Marine uniforms, spotted the overcoat as a piece of German booty. When the two generals emerged from their council they found an Army mule wearing ear pieces cut from the sleeves of Neville's overcoat. Ely had enough presence of mind to blister the mule skinner for looting, and then retired to the pillbox where he could laugh without being heard by the enraged Marine.

The newcomers of the 36th Division carried on in splendid fashion after relieving the veterans of the 2nd, driving the Germans sixteen miles all the way to the Aisne in three days and capturing ten million dollars worth of supplies. But it had taken the combination of hell-for-leather guts and practiced skill of the 2nd Division's Doughboys and Marines to crack the Hindenburg Line bastion of Blanc Mont and pave the way for the German collapse on Gouraud's front.

Chapter

17

Sergeant York

In the Meuse-Argonne sector during the first week of October the Americans had discovered that the hardest fighting always came with the second assault. The first phase of the attack might be compared to a fullback's breaking through a thinly held line of scrimmage when the defense expected an end run. The fullback would now bull into linebackers from the secondary defense rushing up to plug the hole, and it was the second effort that counted. The experience of Major Whittlesey and his "Lost Battalion" was a prime example; after he broke through the front line, the Germans stopped him, plugged the hole, and it took five days for the rest of the division to catch up.

The night before Whittlesey was rescued, October 6–7, a new division, the 82nd, was moving up to relieve the desperately tired 28th Pennsylvanians to the right of the 77th. The 82nd was a medley of backwoodsmen, cotton pickers from Dixie, and city boys reared in tenements. Discretion was never its trademark, despite the caution urged by its commander, Major General George B. Duncan. Duncan was one of the few men ever relieved of command of a division who was later given another command

153

of equal importance. He had led the 77th Division before Alexander had taken it over, and for reasons known only to Pershing had been relieved and sent to Blois, where the A.E.F. had a reclassification camp for officers who had been found unfit for a particular command. On his arrival there, Duncan had spoken out so forcefully, so insistently, and so angrily on his right and qualifications to be given another command that he convinced Pershing that he was "a fighter . . . a fighter . . . a fighter." Given the 82nd Division, in the Meuse-Argonne offensive Duncan proved his worth.

The 82nd moved up to the right of the Argonne Forest and to the left of the Aire River. By the evening of October 7 its leading battalion had carried what was left of enemy positions on Hill 223 beyond the village of Châtel-Chéhéry north of Le Chêne Tondu (see map facing page 136) and was now dug in, two companies having lost two thirds of their riflemen. The leading battalion was holding for the arrival of the next leapfrog battalion, their attacks bent on cutting the north-south railway which supplied German troops in the Argonne and east of the forest.

Captain E. C. B. Danforth, Jr.'s company of the leapfrogs had pushed forward through the night over shell-torn hill country dotted with woods, under a continual rainfall and persistent German shelling. The men moved through mud and rain, all ranks wearing gas masks because of the presence of mustard fumes. Everyone was exhausted by midnight, but Danforth drove his men on because he knew he was behind schedule.

By 5:30 A.M. on the morning of October 8, Danforth was on his jump-off line. He went along his files of tired men, carefully explaining their objective, the railroad two miles ahead whose capture would lead to a German withdrawal. H-hour would be ten minutes past six in the morning, with two attacking waves, staggered about a hundred yards apart, the first wave following a protective barrage. Lieutenant Stewart was the platoon leader on the left, and he would lead one half of his platoon in the first wave. Sergeant Harry M. Parsons, a Brooklyn boy, would lead the second wave with the second half of the platoon. The noncom commanding the squad on the extreme left of Stewart's platoon was Acting Corporal Alvin C. York. York and his men, who would follow Parsons in the second wave, had an open gap on their left flank that separated them from the Pennsylvanians who were about to be relieved.

York had almost become a conscientious objector, one of those who, for religious reasons, do not believe in fighting or killing. In World War II many conscientious objectors served with distinction in various noncombatant capacities, such as orderlies or Corpsmen in the Medical Corps. But in World War I many were sent to prison for their stand. Born and raised in the mountains of eastern Tennessee and taught to believe implicity in the teachings of the Bible, York reported for army service and did his duty as a soldier in doubt and despair. He confided his beliefs to his commanding officers, and they respected his sincerity. The commandment "Thou shalt not kill" was very clear to York, and he felt it should be obeyed. As the Devil was said to be able to do, his battalion commander in a Georgia training camp quoted scripture to his own purpose and finally convinced his troubled young soldier that killing in a just cause was sanctioned by the Bible. The major cited the first six verses of Ezekiel, Chapter 33, ending, "But if the watchman see the sword come, and blow not the trumpet, and the people be not warned; if the sword come, and take any person from among them, he is taken away in his iniquity; but his blood will I require at the watchman's hand."

York was very different from his hard-drinking, two-fisted buddies. He was a teetotaler, a nonsmoker, and he never went out with girls while he was in the service. Until his officers persuaded him that he was justified in breaking the commandment against killing, he observed all ten. In his memoirs he said that his platoon would drink anything in bottles and always hankered to break things, even each other's heads if nothing else was handy. Yet he also said that he had never known the meaning of love until he fought alongside his buddies. The patient concern shown to York by his major is a fine commentary on the American system and the spirit of civilian officers who handled Doughboy draftees. The major might easily have sent York to prison as a conscientious objector, yet he worked manfully not to. It would not have been so in the German or French armies, or anywhere in Europe. (Baron von Steuben, writing from Valley Forge to a friend in the dark hour of the American Revolution, complained that he always had to tell Washington's troops *why* they had to do something. He called it the "genius of this nation" that a private soldier always wanted to understand.)

At daybreak of October 8, Captain Danforth, Lieutenant Stewart, Corporal York, and their men knew they had been seen by the Germans when enemy shells began falling on them. Time and again the Yanks were forced to disperse. One shell scoring a lucky hit wiped out a squad. At 6:10 an American barrage was supposed to begin falling on German positions ahead of the advancing Doughboys, but staff officers had allowed the gunners too little time to come up over roads jammed with ambulances and supply trains, and the only barrage was provided by a giant lieutenant whom Corporal York had never seen before and who appeared with a trench mortar and began to lob his shells into the German defenses. Nevertheless, Captain Danforth kept his commitments. He attacked.

Lieutenant Stewart led his men forward on the left against a German-held hill, but he did not get very far and soon was down with a shattered thigh. He managed to gain his feet and hop a few yards forward until a sniper shot him through the head. The dying Stewart's half of the platoon was now pinned down and digging for life, the ground shaking from hostile mortar fire, the morning air alive with bullets. It was now Sergeant Parsons' turn to do something about these beleaguered men with his half platoon.

Parsons crawled forward to reconnoiter the situation. He noticed that there was dense cover of thicket and woods to the left of the enemy-held hill beyond him, and he decided that by moving his force through this cover he might be able to get behind the hostile machine-gun nests directly ahead. Fanning his men out, Parsons sent his three squads on the left even farther left. These three squads were in the charge of Sergeant Bernard Early, who

had been a song-and-dance man on the vaudeville circuit before
the war. Early's three junior noncoms were Corporals Murray
Savage, William Cutting, and Alvin York. In York's squad were
thirteen privates whose names he never forgot, listing them in
this order: Dymowski, Weiler, Waring, Wins, Swanson, Muzzi,
Beardsley, Konotski, Sok, Johnson, Saccina, Donohue, and Wills.

Sergeant Early was leading a force of sixteen men against the
right flank of a German division of about ten thousand. Somewhere to the right, separated from him by a hill controlled by the
enemy, was Captain Danforth, who was having his own troubles.
And somewhere behind Early was Sergeant Parsons' handful of
men, now also pinned down. Early ordered his men to be silent,
and they set out in single file to stalk the far flank of the German
machine-gun nests. Early alone exposed himself from time to
time to scout the hell ahead by flitting from one clump of brush
to another, his loyal men following.

When the Yanks reached a position where the German gunners
were firing to their right, Early held a council of war. Most of his
Doughboys, knowing they were three hundred yards in advance of
Parsons' pinned-down men and on the flank of the German-held
hill, wanted to surge to the right in a flank attack, but Sergeant
Early overrulled them. He wanted to attack from the rear. The
little column moved on through the brush another three hundred
yards. Early and his men were now in position to attack the rear
of the gunners on the hill opposing Sergeant Parsons and their
buddies.

The sergeant formed his men in three combat teams for the
advance, Early himself boldly leading, Corporal Savage's squad
behind him, Acting Corporal York following Savage, with Corporal Cutting taking the rear guard. The first Germans they saw
were Red Cross men. When called upon to surrender, the enemy
turned and fled into a wood, the riflemen in Savage's squad missing them in a fusillade of shots. Sergeant Early continued on and
presently leaped a little brook, his sixteen men following, and
suddenly found himself in a group of about fifteen German
soldiers, including a major, sitting around in a circle having a

breakfast of bread, jelly, and steaks. Only the German major was armed, and he reached for the sky on command, calling for his men to do likewise. He had no notion of Early's strength.

No sooner had the major surrendered than German fire swept over the group; the Red Cross fugitives seen earlier had sounded the alarm. Early went down with six slugs in his tough frame, Corporal Savage was shot dead, Corporal Cutting went down with wounds, and six others were bleeding, five of them dying on the ground. Corporal York was now in command of eight unwounded men. These eight Doughboys huddled against their captured Germans, all dropping to deep brush, keeping the unarmed prisoners ahead of them for protection. German fire continued to rake the glade, sending steaks and coffee pots flying. York, now the rear guard, wanted to get to his feet, his favorite shooting posture, but to do so would have meant instant death.

About twenty-five yards to his right, on a small rise, York could see clusters of German machine guns, their crews turning the guns to face this unexpected surprise from the rear. The German gunners now sought to depress their machine guns upon York and his eight buddies, unable to raise an elbow, flattened behind their prisoners. Every time a German gunner wanted to aim and fire his gun he had to grab the gun's two handles and raise his head to sight down the barrel. Rarely during this war of trench fighting had a superlative marksman, well concealed in high brush behind a tree trunk and armed with an accurate rifle, been presented with so many targets so close at hand. Corporal York, in his own words, said, "Every time a head done come up, I knocked it down." Like many a Tennessee mountaineer, he could "drive the cross" of a half-inch penciled "X" on a scrap of paper pinned to a tree at a hundred feet, the usual target of the Kentucky and Tennessee riflemen who had killed so many British officers at New Orleans in the War of 1812.

The enemy was now shouting orders, bellowing above the din, their gunners falling the instant they seized the grips of their guns. It was difficult for the Germans to see where this murderous fire originated. They could not hear the shots of York's rifle amidst the chatter of their twenty machine guns, each gun firing bursts of a hundred shots and shearing away underbrush between York and the German positions. But in time, the enemy discovered the approximate location of this astonishingly accurate fire, and they planned a counterattack with bayonets. (Any German attempting to rise and throw a potato-masher grenade would have been shot down instantly.) Six of the enemy, led by an officer, leaped from a trench and, single-file, began a rush at the mountaineer's position.

York's tactics in meeting this team were in the style of a hunter who builds a turkey blind, baits it with a trail of sweet acorns, and then shoots down a file of birds as they advance. An experienced hunter knows that if he shoots the lead bird in the file first, the rest will fly off. York knew that if he shot the lead German first, the others would dive for cover, so he began by killing the hindmost man first, then the next in line and so on up to the leader. In this way none of the charging Germans knew that York's fire was finding its mark. One by one the charging file of six Germans was reduced by York's smoking rifle. But as the Enfield had only a five-bullet clip, York knew he would have to dispose of the sixth German with some other weapon. He was prepared; the little finger of his trigger hand was dangling his cocked Colt .45 automatic in readiness. When the sixth, and leading, man, the German officer, was almost on him, York dropped his rifle and fired a pistol bullet into the German's face.

York now holstered his pistol and thumbed a fresh clip into his Enfield. He was still in command of the situation. The six Germans had not counted on the speed with which York used his pistol; they knew he was firing from a five-clip magazine, and by any ordinary odds at least one of the six should have survived to reach him.

Still the Germans were not convinced, and their machine guns opened fire again. York then continued to split German skulls above the barrels of the machine guns, and he began to call upon the survivors to surrender. He had killed some fourteen more when, in a lull between firing, the captured German major heard

York's demand to surrender, and rose from his hiding place in the brush. Corporal York said he would kill no more if the Germans would surrender. The major blew his command whistle and, with perfect discipline, about thirty men came off the blood-soaked knoll with their hands up, one of them concealing a grenade in his fist. "So I had to tetch him off," York reported to his brigadier. The German major, who had worked in Chicago before the war and spoke English well, asked York if he were English, no doubt having in mind the famous marksmen of the British Regulars. "American," said York. "Good Lord," said the major, who now had the corporal's automatic pistol at his head. He heard the Doughboy demand that he order all his remaining men on the lethal hill to come down with their hands up or the major would suffer irreparable consequences. The rest of the enemy came down. The corporal now had about eighty prisoners. His buddies, the unwounded survivors of Early's three combat teams, no longer pinned down by machine-gun fire, stood up and reported for duty.

York then ordered the German prisoners to head for American lines, carrying Sergeant Early with his five wounds and his broken arm, the body of Corporal Savage, and his surviving wounded men. York marched the German major right in front of him, the Colt .45 pressed against the back of the German's head. There was no chance for the German to lead the Doughboys into a trap, and each time fresh German positions came into view York ordered the major to blow his whistle, and more Germans would join York's growing bag of prisoners.

Eventually the group reached American lines, opening a sizable gap in German defenses, relieving Parsons' and Danforth's men from their perilous situation, and paving the way for an American advance that included cutting the important German railroad. The best thing York said all day was uttered after his battalion commander ordered him to report back to his brigadier, General Lindsay, with his prisoners. "Well, York," said the brigadier, "I hear you have captured the whole damned German Army." "Nossir," said York, "I only have one hundred and thirty-two."

York was promptly awarded the D.S.C. and made a sergeant by

Division, but Pershing added to this. Nothing but the Medal of Honor would suffice for the mountaineer whom Pershing named the outstanding civilian soldier of the A.E.F. and whom Marshal Foch called the outstanding soldier of the war.

York's buddies did not even have time to bask in the glory of his feat, for they were plunging on through the gap he had helped to make. During the four days of October 8 through October 11 progress was made all along the American First Army line. On the right, Bullard's III Corps crossed the Meuse River on its right flank and stormed the heights of the Borne de Cornouiller, known to the Americans as "Corned Willy Hill." German defenses on its steep slopes proved too difficult to capture by a frontal assault, but the Doughboys, having learned some professional discretion by now, dug permanent lines at the base of the hill in preparation for a later attack.

On the American First Army's extreme left flank, the 77th Division drove forward and finally emerged from the north end of the Argonne Forest on October 9–10 (see map facing page 136). In the Meuse-Argonne sector, the Germans' Hindenburg Line was at last beginning to crack.

Chapter

18

Breaking the Kriemhilde Stellung

O<small>N THE MORNING</small> of October 12 an important courier came to the new American supreme headquarters at Souilly to see General Pershing. The courier was Major General Maxime Weygand, Foch's alter ego, a small man of delicate manner, with the porcelain features of a Chinese doll and an almost Mongolian inscrutability. Weygand's errand was to deliver to Pershing a letter from Foch proposing a new plan. To Pershing, it was a bombshell. Foch suggested that the American commander limit his control of his brawny divisions to those that were storming the beetling fortresses in the center of the Meuse-Argonne front, giving two thirds of his men to French generals on the right and the left in order to beef up riddled French divisions. It was Foch's final attempt to take Pershing's army away from him. Under the circumstances it was understandable. While the German defenders had inflicted 75,000 casualties on the Yanks, the French, by comparison, holding down so much more of the front, had suffered 175,000 casualties since mid-August, and this in their fourth year of slaughter.

162

Although Weygand did not say so, Premier Clemenceau had been urging Foch for weeks to ask President Wilson to remove Pershing. Clemenceau had never recovered from the shock of watching the seemingly disorganized Yanks in action when he drove up to inspect Montfaucon after its capture. The Tiger of France had wanted to look through the telescope left behind on the lofty hill by the hated German Crown Prince Rupprecht, who had commanded the German armies on this sector of the front during the Battle of Verdun. But on the single road to the front his limousine had been caught in the bedlam of the Yank 1st Division moving up to relieve the 35th Division moving back, a choking maelstrom of some forty thousand men with all their support. He had sat stalled for hours, badgering his chauffeur, unable to believe what he saw all around him. He had seen field guns fall into craters, and fifty pairs of arms lift them to level road again; exhausted horses dropping dead, replaced by men manning tug ropes. He had witnessed cordons of Doughboys lifting broken down trucks off the road, where they were instantly swarmed upon by mechanics; and ambulances, with lightly wounded soldiers perched on the roofs, intermingled with ammunition convoys and forage trucks. Clemenceau had never gotten to Montfaucon; tiring of the delay, he asked Doughboys to lift his car high in the air and face it to the rear. He had arrived back at Souilly in a dark mood. His idea of a military road was based on practiced French precision, with a truck passing a kilometer marker every five seconds, and he blamed this endless pandemonium of the amateur Americans on Pershing.

Pershing knew of Clemenceau's displeasure; grapevine had alerted him. And now the Tiger had written Foch that he wanted no more arguments about it; this was an order. The French soldier must demand that Wilson recall Pershing in disgrace! It was the ugliest situation in Pershing's career, even though he knew that only if he were stricken with a serious illness would Wilson recall him. Nevertheless, Pershing was prepared, and he met Weygand's visit and Foch's plan that Pershing give up two thirds of his men to French generals on either side of the Meuse-Argonne sector

163

with a counter proposal of his own. When Weygand left Souilly, he carried a letter from Pershing to Foch suggesting that American forces now be divided into two armies, with Pershing as Army Group commander, Liggett in command of one American army and Bullard in command of the other. He also demanded of Foch that he no longer receive orders through Pétain's Group of Armies, as he had been since Saint-Mihiel in early September; he desired an independent army command, equal with Haig and Pétain, reporting only to Foch, the supreme commander of all allied armies. Pershing was summoned the same day to report to Marshal Foch at Bombon.

The scene that followed in the drawing room of an abandoned town house at Bombon resembled a meeting between two skillful prize fighters attended by their seconds—Foch and Weygand versus Pershing and Colonel Carl Boyd, his aide and interpreter. Foch opened the sparring with some light jabs, asking some pointed questions about Wilson's intentions toward continued prosecution of the war in the event of peace talks with the enemy. Pershing parried neatly by replying, "The talk around the White House is that Mr. Wilson will not become involved in long conversations."

"Well," said the old marshal. "And now"—he looked at the Orders of Battle on the wall map—"how are matters progressing on the American front?"

"We have met with very hard fighting," Pershing said quietly. "The Germans are putting up a very determined resistance."

Foch answered this with his first querulous remark. "On all other parts of the front," he said acidly, "the advances are very marked. The Americans are not progressing as rapidly."

Pershing controlled his temper, saying nothing about the 100,000 fresh Doughboys he had contributed to these other fronts, but Foch was ready to start slugging. "I would like to see the Americans advance more rapidly," he said.

The room grew chilly with Pershing's sharp answer. "No army in our place would have advanced farther than the Americans."

Foch became waspish: "Every general is disposed to say the

164

fighting on his front is hardest." Again he waved toward the wall map. "I myself only consider results."

The argument waxed for several minutes, the two soldiers trading charges, insinuations, recriminations, yet neither lost his temper completely; they had too much respect for each other. Pershing on his part admired the Frenchman for the determined fight he had been waging against heavy odds for four long years. And in spite of Clemenceau's opinion, Foch respected this American who had stood up to him in every argument, who had stuck to his principle of holding the Doughboys together and yet had come to Foch's rescue many time by lending him his best divisions.

Finally, the marshal capitulated. "Oh, well," he remarked wearily, "it is a matter of no consequence now. The only thing that matters is results."

At this point Maxime Weygand spoke his only line. "Here is General Pershing's plan for the formation of two armies." Foch did not even look at the plans Weygand placed on the table.

"Ah, yes," the marshal said cheerfully, "I am inclined to grant your request."

As a result of the meeting at Bombon there was a new look to the A.E.F., effective October 12. Pershing was now an Army Group commander co-equal with Haig and Pétain, responsible only to Foch. Liggett took over command of Pershing's old American First Army, whose front would continue to be the Meuse-Argonne sector. Bullard was promoted to command the newly created American Second Army, with a front stretching forty miles from Pont-à-Mousson, east of Saint-Mihiel, to just north of Verdun. Liggett would continue to drive toward Sedan and the important German railway network that passed through it. Bullard's assignment was to push northeast and seize Metz, the Briey iron mines, and the Saar coal basin—the target Pershing had wanted to attack after capturing Saint-Mihiel in mid-September. However, before the Second Army could be organized and the attack fully launched, the Germans would sue for peace.

But there was no peace on the First Army front on October 12 or in the weeks that followed. Liggett, in concert with the French on his left flank, planned a renewed assault on the vicious German defenses remaining in the Meuse-Argonne sector. A good portion of the Kriemhilde Stellung of the Hindenburg line between the north end of the Argonne Forest and the Meuse River was still unbroken, and the date of October 14 was selected to renew the American First Army's attack all along this line.

A look at the map facing page 136, shows the Doughboy divisions that took part in this offensive, most of them new to this campaign, and also reveals something of the complexity of the battle. On the extreme left flank, the untested 78th Division, composed of drafted lads from the mountain hinterlands of New York and New Jersey, relieved the 77th on the evening of October 13 and was poised before the citadel of Grandpré, where the Aire and Aisne rivers join. Beyond Grandpré across the river was the formidable forest, the Bois de Bourgogne, while to the left, separating the Americans from Gouraud's French Fourth Army, were forested hills. An assault on these heavily defended positions was a very difficult assignment, and no one really expected the inexperienced Doughboys of the 78th to capture them. At best the Yanks would exert pressure on the German right flank and prevent the enemy from reinforcing his center.

But Major General James H. McRae, the division commander, had no intention of playing a minor role. He decided to attack with his two infantry brigades along his division front on October 14, with the aim of taking the German positions. Success, however, would not come quickly or easily. On the second day, October 15, the 78th's left brigade captured the farm guarding the village of Talma adjoining the French line, but it took nine more days of fierce fighting and heavy casualties before the brigade captured Talma itself.

Meanwhile, the 78th's right brigade was maneuvering for an assault on Grandpré, perched high above the Aire River. The attack was launched on October 25, and Doughboys and Germans were soon wrestling on the town's terraced roofs. Many German artillery pieces had been rigged with block and tackle to appear, fire, then disappear into hiding places. These guns were very troublesome until some Yanks with a cluster of grenades found them and wiped them out. It was like storming a castle, but the 78th Division took the town on October 27 after two furious days. In all, twelve days of action cost the division a total of five thousand casualties.

In the renewal of the American First Army's assault in the Meuse-Argonne sector on October 14, divisional honors must go to two National Guard outfits, the Rainbows of the 42nd and the German-speaking Michigan and Wisconsin lads of the 32nd. The 32nd had been fighting in the Meuse-Argonne since October 3, the 42nd moving up in time for the October 14 attack. Both divisions were responsible for the center of the First Army's line, and they faced the forested cliffs, fortresses, and the hideous terrain of a wooded hill called the Côte Dame Marie, which guarded the towns of Landres and Romagne, and the Romagne Heights.

On October 13 the 64th Brigade of the 32nd Division, led by Brigadier General Edwin B. Winans, attacked the German defense system of the Côte Dame Marie with its machine guns and one-inch cannons, and took the position on the same day. That night Winans' companion brigade had the town of Romagne and a piece of the woods flanking it.

On Winans' left was Douglas MacArthur's 84th Brigade of the 42nd Rainbows. The 42nd went forward in a blinding rainstorm, yet by nightfall the Rainbows had the other half of Winans' woods, as well as the fiendish and well-nigh unscalable heights of the Côte de Châtillon. It was like a battle royal between teams of homicidal wrestlers armed with lethal weapons. After this the two divisions gained about a mile in two more days of heavy fighting, at the cost of three thousand men in MacArthur's brigade alone. The ground was carpeted with German and American uniforms, bayonets stabbed in earth as headstones for dead Yanks. Pershing cited Winans and MacArthur as deserving of "unstinted praise."

It was October 17 before MacArthur's brigade held the highest ground of Châtillon's deep defense system and could claim possession of a great chunk of the Kriemhilde Stellung. They had now captured the heights before Landres, and many fortress-strong farms with names like la Musarde Farm, la Tuilerie Farm. These positions and those taken by Winans' brigade, fighting just as strongly to the right, were the aces of the Germans' trump cards, the center of their Hindenburg Line defenses. Now the enemy had lost them and were struggling to find any strongpoints they could keep.

On October 17 Liggett pulled out the 42nd and 32nd Divisions to rest, refit, and absorb replacements for his final grand attack against the Freya Stellung. In their place he threw in the 2nd Division and the 89th Division. The 89th was new to war, but its men were resolved to show the boastful Doughboys and Marines of the 2nd that they, too, could whip any man in the saloon.

To the right of the 32nd Division was the 5th "Red Diamond" Division, commanded in mid-October by General John E. Mc-Mahon, but soon to be taken over by the belligerent Hanson E. Ely. In preparation for the October 14 assault, Major General John L. Hines, commander of III Corps, ordered a reconnaissance of the railway and German defenses north of Cunel (see map facing page 136) to see what was ahead of the Red Diamonds, whose nickname, like that of many other divisions, stemmed from their shoulder patch. General McMahon gave the assignment to Major Davis' battalion.

Major Davis had in his ranks the man whom Pershing was to name the outstanding "Old Army" soldier of the war, just as York had earned the status of the outstanding draftee, and Whittlesey the outstanding reservist. Samuel A. Woodfill, Doughboy of Doughboys, was actually the eternal sergeant, the noncom backbone of the army. As a result of heavy casualties and the necessity to promote good men, Woodfill was now a first lieutenant and acting captain. He had grown up in Kentucky listening to the yarns of his grandfather who had served in Lincoln's army in the Civil War. He had a few years of schooling and a term as a woodchopper in Indiana, and then he had enlisted in the Army. He had become an expert marksman, like York, learning with a muzzle-loader. Woodfill had particularly enjoyed his service in Alaska because of the opportunities for hunting big game there. He had six hash marks on his sleeve when he was commissioned, each mark representing three years of honorable service in the ranks.

When the 5th Division had moved up near Cunel on October 10 the Germans had opened up with machine guns and artillery. Woodfill had seen friends dropping all around him, others finding deep cover. Unable to find more than a shallow depression to lie in face down, bullets cutting his protruding pack to pieces, valiant Sam Woodfill thought his time had come then and there. He took the picture of his wife in her wedding dress from a breast pocket and wrote:

October 10, 1918. In case of accident or death it is my last and fondest wish that the finder shall please do me a last and ever-lasting favor to please forward this picture to my Darling Wife, and tell her that I have fallen on the Field of Honor, and departed to a better land which knows no sorrow and feels no pain. I will prepair [sic] a place and be waiting at the Golden Gait [sic] of Heaven for my Darling Blossom. The address Mrs. Samuel Woodfill, 167 Alexandria Pike, Fort Thomas, Kentucky.

Fortunately, Woodfill was saved from his brush with death when American activity on his right attracted the enemy fire, and then fog closed down.

On the morning of October 13 Woodfill set out on the reconnaissance mission ordered by General Hines, the III Corps commander. He led his company past German outposts to a wood, under cover of fog until they came to a field of turnips near a shelled church. As they began crossing the field, the fog lifted and they suddenly came under fire from three machine guns alerted by enemy forward posts. Woodfill, in the lead, could hear the guns firing from three different directions. His top sergeant lay dead beside him. His company was being ripped to pieces. Men flattened out behind any furrows they could find. To move in any direction was to invite death. Woodfill tried to run forward, but the air was screaming with bullets. He chose the nearest shell hole and took stock of the situation, a little sickened by the gas that lingered there.

The first step was to locate the hiding places of the three machine guns. He soon spotted one on the right in the shattered church's tower; a second, to the left, was in the loft of an old barn; the third was dead ahead in a pit concealed by brush. Woodfill's task was more difficult than York's, whose targets had been in a cluster in one direction and considerably closer. But Woodfill, too, knew that for a man to sight down the barrel of a Spandau machine gun he must seize the grips with both hands, hunch his shoulders forward to place his eye to the sight, and expose the upper part of his face. Choosing the church tower gun first, and able to see only its muzzle flash at two hundred yards, Woodfill considered the inches from the gunner's eye to his hairline—about a four-inch bull's-eye—and in the space of a long minute he put five Springfield rifle shots into what he hoped was the center of the ring. After each of the first four shots the gun was momentarily still; it was finally silenced for good after the fifth shot.

Woodfill's next target was the easiest: the gunner in the barn loft. He could see the flash from the barn roof where some tiles had been removed, a favorite haunt for snipers whose rifles were equipped with telescopic sights, but not a good place for a chattering gun. The German in the loft was alone and was operating a light automatic machine gun. Woodfill had no trouble killing him on his first shot. There remained the one ahead in the brush.

Woodfill knew he was now safe from the first two guns, so he took his time moving up from shell hole to shell hole to get closer to this one, while five different gunners took turns trying to kill him. Keeping his automatic pistol ready for instant use, Woodfill, with a single five-cartridge clip in his Springfield, killed in succession the five Germans as each in his turn manned the gun. When a sixth German reared with a bayonet, Woodfill killed him with the pistol. The clearing was now quiet. Woodfill strode forward to count the enemy dead. He had shot six men in the head. Beyond him lay a German first lieutenant, seemingly dead. As

Woodfill bent over him to discover how five Springfield bullets and one Colt's slug could have killed seven men, this brave enemy officer, who had been playing possum, leaped up and seized Woodfill's rifle, at the same time reaching for his Luger pistol. Woodfill had to shoot him through the heart with his Colt.

Woodfill then moved on until he sighted a fourth gun. For once the Germans had not gone deep enough to give their team head-cover. Woodfill had the high ground now, and one by one killed the five men of the gun's crew. Meanwhile, his loyal men, no longer pinned down, were coming forward behind him just as Woodfill encountered three downy-cheeked German boys carrying boxes of ammunition to gunners who would never need them now. A new soldier in the heat of battle would have killed them. Sam Woodfill coolly disarmed them and sent them back to his own men as prisoners.

Woodfill's company, still carrying out their reconnaissance of enemy positions, next tried to cross a muddy ravine, but a fifth machine gun opened up and they were forced to take cover again. Woodfill ruined his uniform then, crawling through foot-deep mud for thirty yards to reduce the angle on the gunners serving it. As usual, there were five of them—gunner, helper, belt-feeder, and two grenadiers. He killed the five of them with his Springfield. When crossfire opened on him, Woodfill jumped into a deep trench and there did the only poor shooting of the day, hitting a German lieutenant in the abdomen with his pistol. As the German fell, Woodfill turned to see another man rushing at him with his bayonet. The Colt was now jammed with mud from the thirty-yard crawl. Woodfill seized an enemy pickax and poled the fellow like an ox, turning in time to see that the lieutenant he had shot in the stomach was sitting up, unconquerable, and weakly raising his Luger. Woodfill split his head with the pickax, and began to free his Colt of the mud.

Sam could not understand at first why, wherever his shadow fell across open sections of the deep, reinforced trench, Germans in the open were firing at him. Then he knew: *He was inside the Kriemhilde Stellung, and they wanted it back.* By now his company—what was left of it—was in the Stellung with him. They had counted the unseen gunners in the church. Yes, there had been five of them, all shot through the head. He sent back his runners, and the battalion recalled him. Major Davis now had a clear picture of enemy dispositions.

The regimental surgeon said that Woodfill's bronchial tubes were so heavily corroded from the lingering mustard gas of the shell holes he had occupied that pneumonia was just around the corner. It was a long time before he was able to leave the hospital and attend the ceremony for the presentation of the Medal of Honor that he had so well earned.

By the end of October Liggett's First Army had cracked the Kriemhilde Stellung on almost every mile of its tortuous defenses from Grandpré east to the Meuse. The I Corps on the left had not yet effected a junction with Gouraud's poilus, but it had advanced almost five miles from its October 14 jump-off line. The biggest penetration had been achieved by the V Corps in the center, thanks to the practiced ferocity of the 42nd and 32nd Divisions in the opening days of the attack and the skill of the 2nd and 89th Divisions. But about the only bright spot for Hines' III Corps on the right was the exploit of Sam Woodfill in the left corner of the corps boundary. Hanson Ely, the new 5th Division commander, finally drove his Red Diamond boys six miles through the Bois des Rappes, which had held them up for three successive days. But to the east, along the Meuse, the Doughboy line had hardly moved forward at all. Across the river the Germans still held the heights of the Borne de Cornouiller, and their shelling of Hines' right flank was merciless and deadly. Liggett had a serious problem with "Corned Willy Hill" that he would have to attend to in the days ahead.

Chapter

19

Breaking the Freya Stellung

Most Germans knew long before mid-October that a German victory in the war was impossible. Some of the top generals realized it after the failure of their July 15 assault in the Second Battle of the Marne, a defeat that shattered hopes built up during the glorious victories of the spring. The Kaiser had come to the same conclusion during the continued setbacks of August; the defeats that followed in September only served to confirm his belief. However, Germany's leaders reasoned that if their armies gave up ground slowly and stubbornly and made every mile advanced by French, British, and American troops a costly and bloody business, the Allies would be more inclined to agree to negotiating peace terms favorable to Germany.

As early as September 29 Generals Ludendorff and Hindenburg decided to urge that the German government put out peace feelers. A few days later Prince Max of Baden, a German diplomat with an international reputation for moderation and honor, was appointed chancellor (Prime Minister), and on October 5 a note pleading for an immediate armistice went out to President Woodrow Wilson. Wilson was chosen rather than one of the other allied leaders because his idealism was well known and the Germans hoped he would be more receptive. He had often spoken of his belief in "peace without victory," by which he meant a peace without vengeance and with justice to victor and vanquished alike. In January of 1918 he had listed Fourteen Points providing for conditions that he deemed necessary for a just and lasting peace. These included such general programs as reduction of arms by all nations, freedom of the seas for all, and, most important, an association of nations to guarantee the protection of all nations, large and small, from attack. This proposed association, later known as the League of Nations, was the unsuccessful forerunner of the United Nations, which was organized after the Second World War.

Wilson had little support from the allied heads of state—Lloyd George of England, Clemenceau of France, and Orlando of Italy— for his high-minded goals. These countries had suffered so much more than the United States from Germany's aggression that their leaders wanted to impose harsh terms in return for a cease-fire, yet they wanted and needed a cease-fire almost as badly as Germany. Pershing, when asked his views, urged that the advance be continued until Germany was invaded and occupied and her army forced to surrender unconditionally. It was his opinion that unless their defeat could be so impressed on all Germans, the allies might "lose the chance actually to secure world peace on terms that would secure its permanence." However, Pershing was first and foremost a soldier, and he followed the wishes as well as the orders of his commander-in-chief, President Wilson.

Unfortunately for German peace hopes, five days after Prince Max's armistice note went to Wilson, German U-boats torpedoed two allied passenger ships and killed many civilians. The President was outraged by these acts, and on October 14 he replied curtly that the allied military leaders would dictate armistice terms to the Germans. He also insisted that Germany institute a more democratic system of government, reduce the authority of the Kaiser, and grant more power to the Reichstag, the German parliament.

On October 23 Wilson dispatched another note to Prince Max

demanding that Germany surrender without any conditions. The disappointed Ludendorff wanted Germany to fight on in the hope that heavy allied losses in attacking the German frontier would change Wilson's mind. But the long series of German setbacks and retreats had discredited Ludendorff; no longer did his opinions carry weight, and on October 26 he was forced to resign. Fearing for his life, he fled in disguise to neutral Sweden.

German fortunes were tottering everywhere. The French and British to the west of the Americans had broken through the Hindenburg Line in front of their armies earlier in October, and their tired troops were driving forward as fast as they could against the retreating foe. (Pershing loaned two more Doughboy divisions to Foch late in October, the 37th and 91st, and they helped a Franco-Belgian army cross the Scheldt River in Belgium.) Germany's Austrian and Turkish allies were on the verge of collapse on their respective fronts (the Turks sued for peace on October 30). There were ominous signs of impending mutiny in the German Navy. Worst of all, the home front was seething with unrest and disaffection. Though the Kaiser had agreed to some democratic reforms—more to please critics at home than to satisfy President Wilson—they were not sufficient to silence growing opposition to him and to the continuation of the war within Germany. The Socialists, who now commanded the major influence in the Reichstag, were demanding a cessation of the war on any terms, and there was increasing pressure on the Kaiser to abdicate his throne. Many German leaders, including Prince Max, were convinced that unless the Kaiser stepped down and the war was ended there would be a revolution within Germany.

As October of 1918 drew to a close, Germany's surrender was only a matter of time, and terms. The collapse of the only strong barriers remaining on the western front, the Freya Stellung and the Borne de Cornouiller, would hasten the end.

Lieutenant General Hunter Liggett, U.S.A., who had no fat above his collar, stood before the last defenses of the Hindenburg Line at daybreak of November 1. His main job was to break the

Freya Stellung, which stood between his troops and the important German railway network that ran through Sedan. In addition, he planned to outflank the Bois de Bourgogne on his left and join up with Gouraud at the village of Boult-aux-Bois six miles north of Grandpré. His third task was to overwhelm the Germans on the Borne de Cornouiller east of the Meuse. These Germans had kept his right wing along the river at a virtual standstill.

Liggett now had an army second to none. It consisted of 550,000 Yanks, nearly all of them now battle-trained, plus 100,000 French. Three corps were poised west of the Meuse ready to strike due north. From left to right, they were Major General Joseph T. Dickman's I Corps, Major General Charles P. Summerall's V Corps, and Major General John L. Hines' III Corps. A fourth corps of French Colonials, augmented by three Doughboy divisions, was east of the river ready to apply pressure to the Borne de Cornouiller.

The only thing Liggett did not have was heavy tanks; America's auto industry had never succeeded in making even one of these simple monsters during World War I, though they mastered the technique to perfection in World War II. Liggett had first-class tactical support from the American aviators overhead, many of whom had been given tours of service with the artillery pieces so that they knew exactly what information the gunners needed to register on enemy targets. The gunners themselves had become precisionists, with the steadfastness of the French and the English and the ardor of the marvelous Canadian batteries. Many artillery regiments, such as those of the 1st Division at Soissons, the 2nd at Blanc Mont, and dozens of others in the Argonne, had remained in line to support green infantry brigades after their own infantry had been relieved. They were swift to exploit targets their infantry wanted them to shell, and to defend an exposed flank with a massive barrage.

Liggett struck the Germans on the dawn of November 1 with prodigious violence, attacking the enemy's center with Summerall's V Corps. Summerall made his first attack on a two-division front, the 2nd Division on his left, the 89th on his right, infantry interlaced with artillery. They wanted the woods and ravines of Barricourt's spiny ridges. If Liggett could bring his heavy guns to Barricourt's eastern ridges, he would command the crossings of the Meuse to his right, and the Germans in the great supply complex of Dun-sur-Meuse would be goners.

The 89th Division called itself the "Middle Wests" and was filled with men from the Canadian border to the Rio Grande, mountain men and trappers, cowboys from the plains, farm lads from the prairies and cornfields, and sundry characters from the ranches and deserts. They were led by Major General William H. Wright, whose tour of the front had been under the tutelage of Pershing himself, and they went into the business of seizing Barricourt's ridges alongside the veteran 2nd Division on their left, determined not to be outdone. By nightfall of November 1, the Middle Wests, keeping pace with the 2nd's Doughboys and Marines, had torn their way five miles through Barricourt's sawtoothed positions, breaking the German infantry line. They were hand-fighting among the enemy's heavy artillery positions when darkness fell.

Frowning Buzancy, just to the left of the 2nd Division's boundary line, was a matter for Dickman's I Corps to settle. Dickman had assigned the taking of Buzancy, six miles distant, to his right-hand division, the 80th. By nightfall of November 1 its patrols were potshooting wherever the bucketed head of a German appeared on Buzancy's southern approaches, and by noon on November 2 the German garrison there—what was left of it—heard the rebel yells of the 80th's southern-born Doughboys. Buzancy-Barricourt was now Liggett's. In less than two days he had broken through the German center and smashed the Freya Stellung, the last barrier of the Hindenburg Line. Enemy infantry between the Yanks and Sedan were no longer capable of establishing a line, and the ten miles Liggett wanted north of Buzancy were his, provided a dogged pursuit was maintained.

Liggett immediately ordered the 77th Division to begin a rapid advance due north to Sedan. (Of all the divisions, the 77th had the best chance of spearheading into Sedan, and Marshal Foch, who secretly wanted French troops to receive that honor, became so alarmed by their progress that he began changing army boundaries almost daily.) Liggett also immediately initiated the second step in his November 1 battle plan, a westward wheel toward Boult-aux-Bois to join up with Gouraud's troops. This task was assigned to the left-hand division in Dickman's corps, the 78th. Its Dough-boys had brutal work ahead of them, for the enemy knew what the Yanks were up to and sent up what they could in the way of artillery and machine guns to reinforce the eastern edge of the Bois de Bourgogne. From this forest the Doughboys were sub-jected to fierce flanking fire, but they drove foward, disregarding their losses, and met Gouraud's poilus on the road winding west from Grandpré to the Aisne on November 5. Gouraud could now cross the Aisne almost unmolested on *his* way to Sedan. A few weeks earlier the New York mountain boys would have been left in the line, but now with reserves to spare Liggett pulled them out as soon as it could be arranged, sending in the 42nd's Rainbows.

On the far right on November 1, Hines' III Corps had a two-pronged mission. The first was to seize Barricourt's easternmost ridges. (If the corps failed to do so, the Middle Wests to the left would then find themselves butchered by flanking enemy how-itzers.) Hines had about fourteen hours of daylight in which to confront these German gunners with the steel of American bayo-nets. He assigned the 90th Division to this task. Its Doughboys called themselves the Alamo Division, and many of them had been taught the art of the fast draw by their pioneer grandmothers. Their shoulder patch was a large red "T" surmounting a rather small "O," showing the relative proportion of Texans to Oklahoma Sooners in the ranks. They, too, had had their baptism in the later stages of the October 14 assault on the Kriemhilde Stellung, fight-ing between the 89th Division and the Red Diamonds of the 5th. Their commander was Major General Henry T. Allen, a timber-topper able to look any of the Texans in the eye. And their 180th Infantry (Texas) Brigade was being led, not just directed, by none other than Ulysses Grant McAlexander, the stubborn colonel of the 3rd Division who had done so much on July 15 to stop the Germans on the Marne. The Alamos set off at dawn November 5, and by nightfall they had covered five miles and stood in triumph on Barricourt's easternmost ridges, sharing the captured German howitzers with the Middle Wests.

Hines' second job was to neutralize Brieulles. This village on the west bank of the Meuse was still in German hands and, supported by German artillery on the Borne de Cornouiller to the east, had been holding up any American progress along the river since September 27. The task of cutting off the town was assigned to the 90th Division's neighbor on the right, the Red Diamonds of the 5th, led by Hanson E. Ely. Tactically, it was the trickiest undertaking of the day. Ely was to attack northeast, cross the Meuse north of Brieulles and circle back and thus cut off the village's German garrison from the Germans east of the river and north to Sedan. Ely proceeded to carry out this difficult operation brilliantly, crossing the Meuse on rafts and bridges improvised by his engineers and catching the Germans in Brieulles and across the river by surprise.

By the night of November 2 Liggett could move forward to the headquarters of his corps and division commanders and listen on field telephones to the bold patrols of his troops. He could also turn his attention to his third task, the capture of the Borne de Cornouiller and its neighboring heights across the river by his fourth corps. Against this last German bastion on the Western Front the French and Yanks had been able to advance only four painful miles since October 8, hacking their way through the enemy trenches and pillboxes on the approaches to these steep slopes in bloody frontal assaults. Now for the first time Liggett had the opportunity to come at the Borne from several directions. He would continue to apply pressure from the south while another column moved in from the east and the main body scaled the hill from the west. At the same time Ely's 5th Division, now across the Meuse above the Borne following its successful maneuver against Brieulles, would cut the northern supply and escape route of the Borne's German garrison.

The Story of the Doughboys

By the evening of November 3, after a last-minute switch in the makeup of this fourth corps, Liggett had approved the French Colonial Corps commander's dispositions for the attack. The U.S. 79th Division, which had taken part in the capture of Montfaucon in September, took up a position east of the Borne, while the 15th French (Colonial) Division was poised along the Meuse just west of it. That night Hanson E. Ely's 5th Division lit the fuse, striking northeast to guarantee the flank and cut off the Borne's defenders from Germans to the north; and while the U.S. 26th Division maintained pressure on the southern face of the hill, Doughboys of the 79th and poilus of the 15th Colonials began their climb to the top.

The Tidewater lads of the 79th had to rely mainly upon Springfields and automatic rifles because of a shortage of trucks for carrying shells and horses for moving the gun teams. The French, better supplied, had horses and artillery support as they began the ascent. The Yanks had to pay with blood and bayonets for their resolve to meet their allies at the top. For four days they battled over ridges and through wooded patches and thickets before they killed the Germans on the summit, Doughboys and poilus meeting there on November 7. The Borne de Cornouiller cost the Americans fifteen thousand casualties. It was the last major effort of the Meuse-Argonne offensive, and its capture marked the successful completion of the three major goals Liggett had set for the American First Army when he sent it forward on November 1.

During these seven critical days, November 1–7, the situation for the Germans had passed the point of any chance for a negotiated peace with terms favorable to Germany. The rapid collapse of the last strong defenses on the Western Front coincided with Austria's surrender to allied forces on the Italian front on November 3. On the same day a mutiny broke out in the German Navy which rapidly developed into a revolution among many German workers on the home front. Stunned and shaken by the turn of events, the Kaiser had taken refuge at Supreme Headquarters at Spa, counting on the German Army to support him against increasing demands that he abdicate. In his absence from Berlin, Prince Max and the Reichstag took control of affairs. In response to a note from President Wilson notifying the German government that General Foch would meet with its representatives to conclude an armistice, an Armistice Commission of German civilians was appointed, headed by Mathias Erzberger, leader of the Center Party.

On November 7 the commission entrained for the French border, and at 7 A.M. on the morning of November 8 its members came face to face with Marshal Foch in his railway car in the French forest of Compiègne. The German delegation got off on the wrong foot by saying it had heard that Foch wished an armistice. The old professor promptly cut them off by saying he desired no armistice. Eventually the harassed German civilians admitted they desired one, whereupon the marshal said they must ask for one. The result of this meeting was German capitulation to all allied demands and an agreement that firing would cease on November 11 at 11 A.M. But November 11 was three days off, and Foch was determined to impress on the Germans that the allied armies were in control and would not let up. He immediately telegraphed the news of the armistice agreement to Haig, Pétain, and Pershing, and he urged them to increase pressure in savage fighting.

Chapter

20

On to Victory

ALTHOUGH there had been peace rumors, few Doughboys below the ranks of division commanders and their staffs knew about the impending armistice. The orders that went out to the infantry on the line during the last few days of the war followed Foch's wishes, and pressure was increased on the retreating enemy. For their part, the German soldiers knew little more than the Yanks that peace was near. It would have made little difference; they were fighting for their own as well as their nation's survival, and as long as the Doughboys kept coming they had no choice but to try to stop them.

Last-ditch fighting in the First Army's center grew so savage that crack outfits such as the 2nd's "racehorse" brigades of Doughboys and Marines were confined to limited gains for two days. Though the enemy now had no established lines, they had gunners and machine gunners galore in almost unassailable hill pockets. And so the relentless Liggett, soon after the 80th, 2nd, and 89th Divisions had broken the line and pushed on several more miles, sent in the Big Red One to expand his center (see map facing page 174). There was never confusion in the fighting, but each division was following Pershing's tactics of pushing on regardless of flank situations. Many villages long since forgotten even by those who fought there were the sites of small but fierce battles and many acts of individual heroism. The veteran Germans, retiring skill-fully, fought in island groups with all their sagacious fury. In order to speed the delivery of ammunition to his rapidly advancing infantry, Pershing ordered ammunition trucks to keep driving at night with lights on, and the drivers took their chances along with the rest of the Doughboys. As a result of this determination and fast pursuit, the 2nd and 89th Divisions broke through German rear guards and reached the southwest bank of the Meuse some ten miles below Sedan on November 4 and 5. One by one the other big, eager Doughboy outfits followed suit, and some began push-ing patrols across the river.

Sometimes there was tragedy in these crossings, for the river was rain-swollen and the enemy was posted on the far bank. A trio in the 89th Division, Sergeant Waldo Hatler and Privates Harold I. Johnson and David B. Barkeley, swam it successfully to look over the tactical situation around Pouilly, which was the division's target on November 10–11. It was a triple Medal of Honor per-formance, but Private Barkeley's decoration was sent to his mother; he drowned on the way back.

Nearer to Sedan, Louis Van Iersal of the 9th Infantry Regiment, 2nd Division—an old buddy of Leo J. Bailey, whose fighting days had been brought to an end when he was wounded by a German shell near Belleau Wood—also won the most coveted award in a remarkable feat. Van Iersal, on a solo intelligence mission in the dead of night, walked into an enemy trap, a river footbridge rigged with a hidden trapdoor that dropped when he stepped on it. As he fell twenty feet into the chilling water, the Germans ignited oil they had poured on the surface and, with this illumination, opened up with machine guns from the east bank. Expecting that any ordinary mortal would swim back to the west bank of the river, enemy gunners searched there with machine gun tracers. But Van Iersal was not an ordinary mortal. He swam *toward* the

183

enemy's side, near Mouzon, climbed out and eavesdropped for a spell, and then swam back with his knowledge of German dispositions.

It was understandable that each of Liggett's division commanders was eager to be the first in Sedan before the war ended. Pershing made the decision, issuing an order that the honor of entering Sedan was to go to the Doughboys of Dickman's I Corps who were closest to the city, the National Guardsmen of the 42nd's Rainbows, and the New Yorkers of the 77th. He added, "assisted on the right by the V Corps." The Big Red One was the left-hand division in the V Corps, located on the Meuse to the right of the 77th, about five miles below Sedan. Officers and Doughboys of the 1st Division immediately interpreted Pershing's phrase as giving them equal right to join the rush. Thousands of them did a left-face and set out for Sedan on the double—foot, horse, and gun—moving for forty-eight hours without their own food or water across the supply routes—the lifelines—of Dickman's neighboring I Corps.

The result was total chaos, and if the enemy had not been near defeat it could have been a disastrous blunder (see map facing page 174). As it turned out, puzzled infantrymen and gunners of the 77th Division in Dickman's I Corps shared field rations and water with a horde of strangers moving across their rear, while General Alexander, their division commander, raged in his headquarters. The horde swept on, moving into the Rainbows' territory. The newly appointed commander of the 42nd Division was Brigadier General Douglas MacArthur, who had come to France as the division's chief of staff, and, as we have seen, later commanded its 84th Brigade. That brilliant officer, moving about as usual near the front line, was wearing his floppy cap, greenish blouse, and glittering boots. Some of the 1st Division Yanks thought he was a German general, fired warning shots, and claimed him prisoner. When the general insisted he was an American, he was told to "tell that to our Intelligence officer, Heinie." West Pointer MacArthur stood patiently until that unfortunate officer arrived, and then proceeded to tell him off.

The situation was further confused when Marshal Foch decreed that the honor of entering Sedan would go to Gouraud's French Fourth Army, and he informed Pershing that the Yank army's western boundary would now be well east of the city. But Gouraud's weary poilus had not been able to keep pace with the eager Doughboys, and the mixture of Rainbows and Big Red One lads was now blocking the French army's route and forcing it to go west of the city. Fortunately, the Germans were in no condition to exploit the situation.

And so, as November 10 dawned, a confused, ferocious mixture of Doughboy divisions was poised on the line of the Meuse. That morning they began crossing the river in force by many means, Foch asking all commanders to launch particularly brutal attacks that day. Doughboy engineers, working out of sight of the Germans on some of the Meuse's tributaries behind American lines, had built seventy-five-man log rafts in only a few days. Other engineers, working the night before, strung pontoon footbridges to the other side of the river. All day the infantry floated across on the rafts or ran over the footbridges, attempting to establish a bridgehead on the other side. There were repulses at many points; the Germans were always professional when they were in strong positions. The assault continued into November 11, and Doughboys were shot off the pontoons of the Meuse up to an hour before the cease-fire order went out at 11 A.M.

Where veterans in the Meuse line were halted in their tracks, forbidden to fraternize with the enemy, they stretched upon the ground, thanked God they were alive, and built their first campfires—feeling ill at ease because no guns were firing anywhere. A man could stand up. In the rear, members of Signal Corps units and artillery batteries could recollect villages they had just passed through, and some men bolted back to these towns to relax in the cafés. Here and there units failed to get the word, and there were random killings.

"I didn't know the war was over until early that evening," said Corporal Sergeant Shaffer, sometime runner to the Truman Battery, whose division was now in Bullard's army on the Metz front. "I only knew the 35th Division was going to fight on the fourteenth, and had spent the day taking down the antennae and lifting heavy things into trucks. We hadn't heard any firing, and it had come on to drizzle around dark. Then we heard a dispatch rider coming hell-bent down the road with his lights out, and we figured the war was still on. When he saw our trucks by the side of the narrow white road in the gloaming, he hit his brakes and the motor bike skidded one way and he slid the other. The engine was running mad, and we figured he'd been killed. But God looks after drunks. He jumped up, threw us a copy of the Paris *Herald* from his pouch, shouted, 'The damn war is over,' grabbed the bike . . . and was gone. We knew where he was going to, and we took off for it. When we got there . . . the street was already knee-deep in bottles . . . guys walking around in their sock feet begging other guys not to break any more . . . I came to sleeping on some porch steps. An old farm wife in a starchy white hood was offering me a hot jug of our java. '*Bone Joor*, *M'Soor*,' she said, and just beamed. Hell. You'd have thought I won the war."

Far to the west in Flanders, Lieutenant Grantland Rice, a famous sports writer before and after the war, said that everyone in the 37th Division got drunk on Flemish hospitality. In Italy, a token force of Doughboys, the 332nd Infantry Regiment of the 83rd Division that had been fighting with the Italian Army, began their march into conquered Austria. Above them flew an American aviator, Captain Fiorello La Guardia, destined to be a great mayor of New York City some twenty years later. Aviators in France outdid themselves in loops and rolls celebrating victory. On the Swiss border, Lieutenant Thomas Hitchcock, Jr., seventeen years old now and later to be a world-famous polo player, had crossed Germany on foot after escaping from a prison train. As he crawled beneath the wire, grinning Swiss guards informed him the war had just ended. Sergeant York, in the city of Nancy, said every drunken Doughboy there had a girl on his arm when he, after having a sandwich and a lemonade, went to bed around sundown.

Paris was wild; on the way to see Clemenceau the next day, Pershing's car took two hours to cross the Place de la Concorde to the Hotel Crillon. London had its great show, and New York City went on a binge, but there was very little rejoicing in Berlin, only relief that the killing was over. The Kaiser at last was gone. Before dawn on November 10 he had boarded the imperial train and gone to take refuge in Holland, having renounced the throne for himself and his family. He left behind a nation in turmoil.

The British Isles mourned three quarters of a million dead, about 625,000 of these killed in battle. More than a million uniformed French were in battlefield cemeteries. The Germans had seen about two million of their men killed between the Russian and Western fronts, on Balkan mountains and even in sunny Palestine, in the four years it took the rest of the world to whip them. The Germans' main ally, the Austro-Hungarian Empire, lost about a million men, and would soon disappear as a nation on the world's maps and be replaced by such individual countries as Austria, Czechoslovakia, Hungary, and Yugoslavia. No one ever knew what Russian deaths totaled. It was anyone's guess; possibly three million in battle and seventeen million more from wounds, disease and starvation in the "war to end war." The Doughboys, fighting for less than a year, buried only eighty-three thousand battle casualties, though forty thousand more died from other causes.

There was no stillness on the Yank fighting lines, as there had been on the last battlefield of the Civil War. It was a matter of noisy laughter, of men too weary to shed tears. "I saw battle-corpses," Walt Whitman had written after the Civil War,

> . . . myriads of them, and the white skeletons of the young men, I saw them, I saw the debris and the debris of all the slain soldiers of the war, but I saw they were not as I had thought, they themselves were fully at rest, they suffered not, the living remained and suffered, the mother suffered, and the wife and the child and the musing comrade suffered, and the armies that remained suffered.

Epilogue

The Doughboys would now be going home. There were 190,000 wounded, and some of them would have to be carried aboard hospital ships on stretchers. Others would walk up gangplanks with arms in plaster casts or heads wrapped in bandages. The non-wounded would be shipped on transports with their outfits when their turn came. General Harbord, in command of the Service of Supply since July, would have his hands full finding enough transports for nearly two million Yanks, and it would take time. In the belief that idle hands lead to mischief, Pershing kept Doughboy noses to the grindstone, drilling them endlessly outdoors in all manner of military arts through the cold winter months. All sorts of diversions were introduced to keep the men occupied: boxing matches (Gene Tunney, a Marine, and soon to win the heavyweight title from Jack Dempsey, won several bouts against other servicemen in France); football games between regiments and divisions; plays, musicals, and reviews staged by the men themselves and by visiting professionals. Some divisions were assigned to German occupation duty and marched off to the Rhine.

Before many of the Doughboys could leave for the States, President Woodrow Wilson came to France. He arrived in December to meet with the leaders of England, France, and Italy to work out details of the peace. He brought with him all his hopes and plans for a just and lasting settlement, and he was due to be frustrated and disappointed at almost every turn. The treaty that was finally drawn up six months later, after endless days and nights of discussion, disagreement, and compromise was a far cry from the idealism of Wilson's Fourteen Points. In all respects the Treaty of Versailles, which Germany had no choice but to sign, was a vengeful document full of unrealistic demands. It stripped Germany of her overseas colonies and divided them among the allies. Alsace-Lorraine was ceded to France, and portions of Prussia were given to the newly created country of Poland. Most serious, it insisted that Germany make enormous payments—reparations —over a period of years to the Allies for damages, and then severely limited her overseas commerce and the goods she needed to produce and sell to make such payments. Of course, these reparations were never paid. Instead of helping to bind up Europe's wounds, the Treaty of Versailles created much bitterness and helped to sow the seeds of World War II.

The final, tragic irony for President Wilson was yet to come. Outmaneuvered by the Allied leaders in his desire for a peace without vengeance, forced to compromise on point after point, he at last secured their approval for one of his most cherished dreams, a League of Nations. Then, exhausted from his efforts, he sailed for home, only to have the U.S. Senate, controlled by some of his bitterest political enemies, vote against permitting the United States to participate in the League.

The failures of the Treaty of Versailles cannot detract from the tremendous sacrifices and accomplishments of the Doughboys, who did so much to bring an end to the First World War only seventeen months after the first Yank soldier stepped ashore in France. The battles they fought have become legends in American history along with great battles of other American wars. Throughout the country, wherever there is state or regional pride in great deeds of the past, there are monuments honoring the contributions

189

of local regiments and paying respects to those who fell at Seiche-prey or Cantigny; at Belleau Wood, the Marne, Soissons; in the seemingly endless battles in the Aisne-Marne salient; at Saint-Mihiel, Saint-Quentin, Blanc Mont, or in the Meuse-Argonne.

Nor have the sacrifices of the Doughboys been forgotten by the Allies. There is a small, brick-walled cemetery in Flanders, not far from Brussels, that holds the remains of 368 Doughboys who fell nearby. The line carved above their chapel door is a fitting epitaph for these Yanks who gave their lives in a just cause on foreign soil: GREET THEM EVER WITH GRATEFUL HEARTS

Appendix

AMERICAN DIVISIONS SENT TO EUROPE

THEIR DATES OF ARRIVAL, CASUALTIES AND LOCALITIES
FROM WHICH ORIGINALLY RAISED

REGULAR ARMY DIVISIONS

Div.	Date Div. Hdqrs. arrived in France	Battle deaths and died of wounds	Wounded	Locality from which division was originally raised (Many divisions were reorganized prior to sailing for Europe)
1	June 26, 1917	4,996	17,324	At large.
2	. . . .	1 5,155	2 18,080	At large. (Included one brigade of marines.) Division formed in France in 1917.
3	Apr. 4, 1918	3,401	12,000	At large.
4	May 17, 1918	2,903	9,917	Do.
5	May 1, 1918	2,120	6,996	Do.
6	July 22, 1918	68	318	Do.
7	Aug. 11, 1918	287	1,422	Do.
8	Nov. 9, 1918	. . . . .	. . . . .	At large. (Part arrived in France just prior to Armistice.)

NATIONAL GUARD DIVISIONS

26	Oct. 28, 1917	2,281	11,383	New England.
27	May 31, 1918	1,829	6.505	New York.
28	May 18, 1918	2,874	11,265	Pennsylvania
29	June 28, 1918	1,053	4,517	New Jersey, Virginia, Maryland, Delaware, District of Columbia.
30	May 24, 1918	1,641	6,774	Tennessee, North Carolina and South Carolina.
31	Oct. 15, 1918	. . . .	. . . .	Georgia, Alabama and Florida. (Became 7th Depot Division.)
32	Feb. 20, 1918	3,028	10.233	Michigan and Wisconsin.
33	May 24, 1918	993	5,871	Illinois.
34	Oct. 3, 1918	. . . .	. . . .	Nebraska, Iowa, North Dakota, South Dakota and Minnesota. (Personnel used as replacements.)
35	May 11, 1918	1,298	5,998	Missouri and Kansas.
36	July 30, 1918	591	1,993	Texas and Oklahoma.
37	June 23, 1918	1,066	4,321	Ohio.
38	Oct. 4, 1918	. . . .	. . . .	Indiana, Kentucky and West Virginia. (Personnel used as replacements.)
39	Aug. 27, 1918	. . . .	. . . .	Arkansas, Mississippi and Louisiana. (Became 5th Depot Division.)
40	Aug. 24, 1918	. . . .	. . . .	California, Colorado, Utah, Arizona and New Mexico. (Became 6th Depot Division.)
41	Dec. 31, 1917	93	315	Washington, Oregon, Montana, Idaho, Wyoming, Colorado, North Dakota, South Dakota, New Mexico and District of Columbia. (Became 1st Depot Division.)
42	Nov. 1, 1917	2,810	11,873	Composite division from 26 States and District of Columbia.

NATIONAL ARMY DIVISIONS

76	July 16, 1918	4	22	New England and New York. (Became 3d Depot Division.)
77	Apr. 13, 1918	2,110	8,084	New York City and vicinity.
78	June 8, 1918	1,530	5,614	New York, New Jersey and Delaware.
79	July 16, 1918	1,517	5,357	Pennsylvania, Maryland and District of Columbia.
80	May 30, 1918	1,241	4,788	Virginia, West Virginia and Pennsylvania.
81	Aug. 16, 1918	248	856	North Carolina, South Carolina and Florida.
82	May 13, 1918	1,413	6,664	Georgia, Alabama and Tennessee.
3 83	June 17, 1918	67	257	Ohio and Pennsylvania. (Became 2d Depot Division.)
84	Sept. 25, 1918	. . . .	. . . .	Kentucky, Indiana, Illinois. (Personnel used as replacements.)
4 85	Aug. 10, 1918	145	281	Michigan and Wisconsin. (Became 4th Depot Division.)
86	Sept. 23, 1918	. . . .	. . . .	Illinois and Wisconsin. (Personnel used as replacements.)
87	Sept. 9, 1918	. . . .	. . . .	Arkansas, Louisiana, Mississippi and Alabama.
88	Sept. 4, 1918	20	58	North Dakota, Minnesota, Iowa and Illinois.
89	June 21, 1918	1,466	5,625	Kansas, Missouri, South Dakota, Nebraska, Arizona, Colorado and New Mexico.
90	July 7, 1918	1,496	6,053	Texas and Oklahoma.
91	July 23, 1918	1,454	4,654	Montana, Nevada, Wyoming, Utah, Washington, Oregon, California and Idaho.
92	June 19, 1918	182	1,465	Colored troops (various states).
93	Mar. 5, 1918	591	2,943	Colored National Guard and other troops (various states) four infantry regiments only.
Other troops........		976	2,802	
		52,947	202,628	

1 Includes 2454 Marine Corps and 18 Navy serving with the Marine Corps.
2 Includes 8894 Marine Corps and 123 Navy serving with the Marine Corps.
3 332d Infantry of this division went to Italy in July 1918 and saw active service.
4 339th Infantry of this division served at Archangel, Russia, for a time.

191

AMERICAN DIVISIONS SENT TO EUROPE

THEIR POPULAR NICKNAMES, COMPOSITION, DAYS IN MAJOR OPERATIONS, DAYS IN SECTOR, MILES ADVANCED, PRISONERS CAPTURED, PRISONERS LOST AND REPLACEMENTS RECEIVED

Columns under *Numeral Designation of Units in Division*: Inf. Brigades, Inf. Regiments, F.A. Brig., F.A. Regts., Engr. Rgt., M.G. Bns. Columns under *Days in Front Line*: Training in Line, Sector, Battle, Total.

Div.	Popular Nickname	Inf. Brigades	Inf. Regiments	F.A. Brig.	F.A. Regts.	Engr. Rgt.	M.G. Bns.	Training in Line	Sector	Battle	Total	Approx. No. of Miles Advanced	Prisoners Captured	Prisoners Lost	Replacements Received	Div.
1	(Big Red One)[1]	1, 2	16, 18, 26, 28	1	5, 6, 7	1	1, 2, 3	47	148	28	223	32	6,469	152	30,206	1
2	(race-horse brigades)[1]	3, 4	9, 23, **5**, **6**	2	12, 15, 17	2	4, 5, **6**	58	48	33	139	37	12,026	157	35,343	2
3	Marne	5, 6	4, 7, 30, 38	3	10, 18, 76	6	7, 8, 9	0	39	50	89	25	2,240	314	24,033	3
4	Ivy (Ivy Leafs)	7, 8	39, 47, 58, 59	4	13, 16, 77	4	10, 11, 12	0	11	36	47	15	2,756	72	19,559	4
5	Red Diamond	9, 10	60, 61, 6, 11	5	19, 20, 21	7	13, 14, 15	33	39	32	104	18	2,356	100	12,611	5
6	None	11, 12	51, 52, 53, 54	6	3, 11, 78	318	16, 17, 18	6	37	0	43	0	12	3	2,784	6
7	None	13, 14	55, 56, 34, 64	7	8, 79, 80	5	19, 20, 21	0	33	0	33	1	69	20	4,112	7
8	Pathfinder	15, 16	12, 62, 8, 13	8	2, 81, 83	319	22, 23, 24							1		8
26	Yankee	51, 52	101, 102, 103, 104	51	101, 102, 103	101	101, 102, 103	42	118	45	205	23	3,148	457	14,411	26
27	New York (Orions)	53, 54	105, 106, 107, 108	52	104, 105, 106	102	104, 105, 106	25	0	32	57		2,357	229	5,255	27
28	Keystone	55, 56	109, 110, 111, 112	53	107, 108, 109	103	107, 108, 109	14	44	44	102	7	921	732	21,717	28
29	Blue and Gray	57, 58	113, 114, 115, 116	54	110, 111, 112	104	110, 111, 112	13	46	23	82	6	2,187	68	4,977	29
30	Old Hickory	59, 60	117, 118, 119, 120	55	113, 114, 115	105	113, 114, 115	33	1	35	69	4	3,848	75	2,384	30
31	Dixie	61, 62	121, 122, 123, 124	56	117, 118, 119	106	116, 117, 118							2		31
32	Iron Jaws (*Gemütlichkeit boys*)	63, 64	125, 126, 127, 128	57	119, 120, 121	107	119, 120, 121	25	37	38	100	22	2,153	161	20,140	32
33	Prairie	65, 66	129, 130, 131, 132	58	122, 123, 124	108	122, 123, 124	27	33	38	98	22	3,987	127	5,415	33
34	Sandstorm	67, 68	133, 134, 135, 136	59	125, 126, 127	109	125, 126, 127									34
35	None	69, 70	137, 138, 139, 140	60	128, 129, 130	110	128, 129, 130	37	43	30	110	7	781	167	10,605	35
36	Lone Star	71, 72	141, 142, 143, 144	61	131, 132, 133	111	131, 132, 133	0	0	19	19	13	549	24	3,397	36
37	Buckeye	73, 74	145, 146, 147, 148	62	134, 135, 136	112	134, 135, 136	7	57	13	77	19	1,495	23	6,282	37
38	Cyclone	75, 76	149, 150, 151, 152	63	137, 138, 139	113	137, 138, 139							2		38
39	Delta	77, 78	153, 154, 155, 156	64	140, 141, 142	114	140, 141, 142							2		39
40	Sunshine	79, 80	157, 158, 159, 160	65	143, 144, 145	115	143, 144, 145							3		40
41	Sunset	81, 82	161, 162, 163, 164	66	146, 147, 148	116	146, 147, 148							4		41
42	Rainbow	83, 84	165, 166, 167, 168	67	149, 150, 151	117	149, 150, 151	31	100	45	176	34	1,317	112	17,253	42
76	None	151, 152	301, 302, 303, 304	151	301, 302, 303	301	301, 302, 303							3		76
77	Metropolitan	153, 154	305, 306, 307, 308	152	304, 305, 306	302	304, 305, 306	25	31	63	119	44	750	403	12,728	77
78	Lightning (White Lightnings)	155, 156	309, 310, 311, 312	153	307, 308, 309	303	307, 308, 309	0	18	22	40	13	432	123	3,190	78
79	Liberty	157, 158	313, 314, 315, 316	154	310, 311, 312	304	310, 311, 312	0	29	18	47	12	1,077	80	6,246	79
80	Blue Ridge	159, 160	317, 318, 319, 320	155	313, 314, 315	305	313, 314, 315	16	0	31	47	24	1,813	100	4,495	80
81	Stonewall	161, 162	321, 322, 323, 324	156	316, 317, 318	306	316, 317, 318	14	18	5	37	3	101	51	1,984	81
82	All American	163, 164	325, 326, 327, 328	157	319, 320, 321	307	319, 320, 321	17	58	30	105	11	845	240	8,402	82
83	Ohio	165, 166	329, 330, 331, 332	158	322, 323, 324	308	322, 323, 324							3		83
84	Lincoln	167, 168	333, 334, 335, 336	159	325, 326, 327	309	325, 326, 327							1		84
85	Custer	169, 170	337, 338, 339, 340	160	328, 329, 330	310	328, 329, 330							18		85
86	Black Hawk	171, 172	341, 342, 343, 344	161	331, 332, 333	311	331, 332, 333									86
87	Acorn	173, 174	345, 346, 347, 348	162	334, 335, 336	312	334, 335, 336									87
88	Cloverleaf	175, 176	349, 350, 351, 352	163	337, 338, 339	313	337, 338, 339	22	21	0	43	0		9	734	88
89	Middle West	177, 178	353, 354, 355, 356	164	340, 341, 342	314	340, 341, 342	0	54	28	82	30	5,061	25	7,669	89
90	Alamo	179, 180	357, 358, 359, 360	165	343, 344, 345	315	343, 344, 345	0	43	26	69	17	1,876	81	4,437	90
91	Wild West	181, 182	361, 362, 363, 364	166	346, 347, 348	316	346, 347, 348	0	6	17	23	21	2,412	28	12,530	91
92	Buffalo	183, 184	365, 366, 367, 368	167	349, 350, 351	317	349, 350, 351	7	56	0	63	5	38	17	2,920	92
93	None[2]	185, 186	369, 370, 371, 372											4		93

Marine units, all in 2nd Division, in bold face type.
[1] Unofficial nickname used in *The Doughboys.*
[2] Never operated as a division.

Miles of Western Front occupied by American and Allied forces in 1918

Date (1918)	American	British	French [1]	Belgian	Total
Jan. 31	6	116	323	23	468
Mar. 20	17	116	312	23	468
Mar. 30	19	92	353	23	487
Apr. 10	31	92	348	23	494
Apr. 30	34	83	358	23	498
May 30	23	83	393	23	522
June 10	36	83	389	23	531
June 20	65	83	360	23	531
July 10	62	92	354	23	531
July 20	55	92	362	23	532
July 30	68	92	318	23	501
Aug. 10	79	93	277	23	472
Aug. 20	85	93	276	23	477
Aug. 30	90	87	262	23	462
Sept. 10	98	87	241	23	449
Sept. 30	82	83	258	28	451
Oct. 10	101	83	244	15	443
Oct. 30	79	68	248	15	410
Nov. 11	83	70	214	25	392

[1] The sections of the front which were held by Italian and Portuguese divisions are included with French.

Maximum number of miles of front line held at one time by American units:

101 miles on October 10, 1918.

Total length of the Western Front:

Oct. 1914—468 miles.
July 17, 1918—532 miles.

Maximum number of American divisions that saw action during any one week:

29 during second week of October 1918.

Approximate average actual strength of the various combat divisions on the Western Front during the year 1918:

American 25,500
British 11,800
French 11,400
German 12,300

Greatest number of Americans that arrived in Europe during any single month:

313,410 during the month of July 1918.

Actual combat strength of the A.E.F.:

Mar. 21, 1918	162,482
May 27, 1918	406,844
Aug. 10, 1918	822,358
Sept. 12, 1918	999,602
Oct. 12, 1918	1,078,190
Nov. 11, 1918	1,078,222

These figures include only combat troops and exclude the troops in the S. O. S., headquarters, schools, hospitals, liaison service and other special services.

Cumulative arrivals in Europe of American military personnel for the A.E.F.:

By May 31, 1917	1,308
By June 30, 1917	16,220
By July 31, 1917	20,120
By Aug. 31, 1917	39,383
By Sept. 30, 1917	61,927
By Oct. 31, 1917	92,265
By Nov. 30, 1917	129,623
By Dec. 31, 1917	183,896
By Jan. 31, 1918	224,655
By Feb. 28, 1918	254,378
By Mar. 31, 1918	329,005
By Apr. 30, 1918	434,081
By May 31, 1918	667,119
By June 30, 1918	897,293
By July 31, 1918	1,210,703
By Aug. 31, 1918	1,473,190
By Sept. 30, 1918	1,783,955
By Oct. 30, 1918	1,986,618
By Nov. 11, 1918	2,057,675

Combat strength of A.E.F. by branch of service at the time of the Armistice:

Infantry and M. G. Battalions .	646,000
Engineers	81,600
Signal Corps	21,300
Air Service	34,800
Artillery	278,500
Tank Corps	10,200
Amm. Trains, Q. M., etc. . .	70,800
Medical Department . . . . [1] 152,300
Cavalry	6,000
Ordnance . . . . [1] 22,900

[1] Including those on duty in the Services of Supply.

Appendix

Percentage of total strength in various branches of the A.E.F., Nov. 1918:

	Officers; % of total	Enlisted Men; % of total
Infantry	23.83	32.40
Engineers	8.69	12.68
Field Artillery	10.91	11.18
Casuals (all branches)	3.39	10.81
Medical Dept. (Army)	18.46	7.26
Quartermaster Corps	6.33	7.16
Coast Artillery Corps	4.00	3.78
Air Service	7.30	3.11
Ammunition Trains	1.47	2.48
Signal Corps	1.63	1.83
Supply Trains	1.02	1.61
Ordnance Department	1.53	1.16
Marines	0.75	0.96
Headquarters Troops	0.21	0.78
Military Police	0.49	0.67
Hdqrs. Detachments	0.00	0.55
Tank Corps	0.91	0.50
Cavalry	0.25	0.29
Postal Express Service	0.15	0.15
Medical Dept. (Navy)	0.07	0.02
G.H.Q. and General Staff	8.49	0.00

Total strength of A.E.F. on Nov. 11:

Its total strength was 1,981,701, in which were included 32,385 marines.

Number of civilians employed by A.E.F.:

42,644 at the time of the Armistice.

Greatest number of American soldiers in hospitals in Europe at any one time:

190,564 men on November 7, 1918.

Provisions for hospitalization in A.E.F.:

On November 11, 1918, there were 192,844 normal beds, which could have been increased in an emergency to 276,-547. There were 153 base hospitals, 66 camp hospitals, 12 convalescent camps, 21 hospital trains and 6,875 ambulances.

The information in this Appendix is based on material in *American Armies and Battles in Europe*, prepared by American Battle Monuments Commission (U.S. Government Printing Office, 1927 and 1938).

Index

Index

Index

Index

Index

Format by Erle Yahn
Set in Linotype Monticello
Composed, printed and bound by The Haddon Craftsmen, Inc.
HARPER & ROW, PUBLISHERS, INCORPORATED